The First Dukes of Normandy

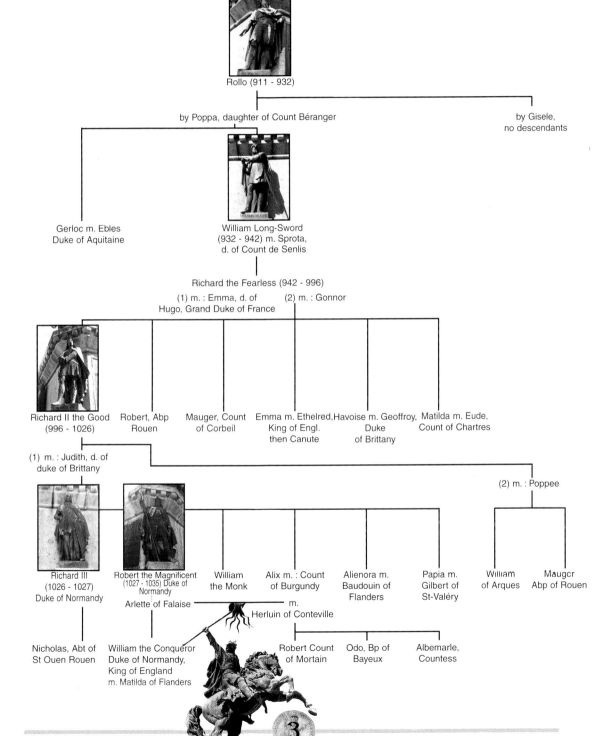

Rollo (911 - 932)

by Poppa, daughter of Count Béranger

by Gisele,
no descendants

Gerloc m. Ebles
Duke of Aquitaine

William Long-Sword
(932 - 942) m. Sprota,
d. of Count de Senlis

Richard the Fearless (942 - 996)

(1) m. : Emma, d. of
Hugo, Grand Duke of France

(2) m. : Gonnor

Richard II the Good
(996 - 1026)

Robert, Abp
Rouen

Mauger, Count
of Corbeil

Emma m. Ethelred,
King of Engl.
then Canute

Havoise m. Geoffroy,
Duke
of Brittany

Matilda m. Eude,
Count of Chartres

(1) m. : Judith, d. of
duke of Brittany

(2) m. : Poppee

Richard III
(1026 - 1027)
Duke of Normandy

Robert the Magnificent
(1027 - 1035) Duke of
Normandy

William
the Monk

Alix m. : Count
of Burgundy

Alienora m.
Baudouin of
Flanders

Papia m.
Gilbert of
St-Valéry

William
of Arques

Mauger
Abp of Rouen

Arlette of Falaise ——————— m.
Herluin of Conteville

Nicholas, Abt of
St Ouen Rouen

William the Conqueror
Duke of Normandy,
King of England
m. Matilda of Flanders

Robert Count
of Mortain

Odo, Bp of
Bayeux

Albemarle,
Countess

3

Illegitimacy, a Ducal tradition

Although converted to Catholicism the Dukes of Normandy had retained a "Danish" marriage tradition : in addition to their lawful wife they kept in their household a "sweetheart" the offspring of which were placed on the same footing as their legitimate children.

Robert the Magnificient was no exception when he took Arlette Vertpré, a tanner's daughter from the Town, to live at the Castle with him at Falaise. It was there, one Christmas evening in 1027 that little William was born.

When Duke Robert decided to go off to the Crusades he introduced to his followers his son and heir, not quite eight years old : a Natural infant !

Throughout his life William suffered on this account.

In 1052 at Alencon when the troops of the Town rallied to the Duke of Anjou his enemy, they shouted from the ramparts : "la piel! la piel!" (the hide, an allusion to the trade of his maternal grandfather), exciting the Duke's anger. The latter, victorious, raised the siege and had their arms and legs cut off.

ON THIS SPOT

WHEN BLOOMED THE FIRST FLOWERS OF SPRING
IN THAT YEAR OF GRACE MXXVII
ROBERT THE MAGNIFICENT
DUKE OF NORMANDY, MASTER OF FALAISE
RETURNING ONE EVENING FROM THE CHASE
ESPIED ARLETTE THE TANNER'S DAUGHTER

IN HUE, SHE LOOKED
MORE DELICATE THAN THE ROSE OR MAYFLOWER
AND BLANCHING IN THE STREAM
THAT SPOUTED FROM THIS FOUNTAIN
SOFT RAIMENT AND FINE LINEN

ROBERT LOST HIS HEART TO HER LOVELINESS
AND BADE HER TO HIS CASTLE COME
MOUNTED ON A PALFREY
THITHER WITH JOY HE TOOK HER TO THE VERY KEEP

COME CHRISTMAS, IT CHANCED WAS BORN A SON
WILLIAM
THE CONQUEROR, DUKE OF NORMANDY
THEN KING OF ENGLAND
AFTER THE BATTLE OF HASTINGS MLXVI

Brandishing their arms, menacing, perhaps to do injury, these warriors from a 12th century Bible in the likeness of those on top of the ramparts of Alencon (Orne in 1052), jeered at William to the point of unleashing one of his most terrible fits of anger ever known of him. When captured he had the hands and feet of the defenders cut off. *Bib. mun. Dijon. ms 14 fol. 13v*

Right-hand page : Views of the Chateau at Falaise built on a rocky spur

In his youth, William had to confront the "Richardists" who were hostile to him. They were his own cousins or uncles, descendants of Richard I or Richard II, some of whom were illegitimate like himself, and whom in turn claimed the Dukedom.

They would stop at nothing to achieve their aim. Gilbert de Brionne, William's tutor, was murdered in the little Duke's bedroom.

Later on, William narrowly escaped from a trap, laid by Guy of Burgundy.

These rivalries often ended in revolts, like that of William of Eu, then later, that of William of Arques.

All these uprisings and attempts to revolt were put down severely by William, generous as he was with his friends, he was cruel to traitors.

William Werlenc, Count of Avranches and Mortain found this to his cost. William forced him into exile when he learnt of his ambitions. William Werlenc returned to Sicily, never again to see Mortain, his title being given to Robert, the Duke's half-brother.

The most dangerous revolts against William, putting his life and throne at risk, were by Guy of Burgundy and William of Arques.

1046. Escape on horseback from the Bessin

The young Duke of Normandy was staying near Valognes and engaged in his favouvrite sport, hunting.

At dead of night he was warned that a plot had been hatched against him by Guy of Burgundy and Neil II of Saint Sauveur. William, taken aback, had time only to mount a horse and take flight. His disconcerted departure took him to Ryes and the lands of his old friend Hubert who had a fresh horse saddled for him and provided an escort. That the conspirators were set on taking his life is certain. The route he chose led to safety : Falaise. William was later to raise the surface of this Roman road in stone in token of his gratitude, whence its name "chemin chaussé" by which it is still known.

These plaques : on a street in Asnelles (above) and a street in Ryes (right) mark the starting points of Guillaume's ride to Falaise

"NEAR THIS SPOT AT DAWN IN JANUARY 1047 OCCURRED THE HISTORIC "RENCONTRE" BETWEEN WILLIAM DUKE OF NORMANDY AND HUBERT OF RYES HIS VASSAL, THANKS TO WHOM HE ESCAPED HIS VENGEFUL REBELS BENT ON KILLING HIM AND REACHED HIS CHATEAU AT FALAISE SAFE AND SOUND"

1047. The Battle of Val-es-dunes

Guy of Burgundy, more than ever determined, had marshalled the fine flower of "Noblesse" in the Cotentin and Bessin. All had taken oath at Bayeux to help William's cousin to seize the ducal throne, they numbered over a thousand, under the orders of Hamon le Dentu (Seigneur of Creully), Raoul Tesson (of Thury Harcourt), Ranulfe of Briquessard (Viscount of Bayeux), Grimoult du Plessis, Neil II of Saint Sauveur and Guy of Burgundy himself. They determined on a final thrust.

The young Duke of Normandy, remembering that previously, his father had had recourse to the King of France for help, pleaded his cause with his suzerain. Henry I agreed : he raised an army of several thousand soldiers who joined those of William at Val-es-dunes near Bellengreville to face the rebels.

The battle that followed was terrible. "The Cry of Dex aïe" (By God's help) from William's side, "Thor aïe" (By Thor's help) was the answering battle cry from the rebel barons.

The knights pressed forward, lances to the fore. Arms and horses clashed under the oppressive heat of the day, the 10th of August. The King of France bit the dust but managed to regain his saddle.

Monument at Val-es-dunes South of Caen between Chicheboville and Bellengreville.

Outmatched, Hamon le Dentu and Ranulfe of Bayeux were killed, their men fled, many were taken prisoner.

William and Henry I were victorious, the revolt put down. The leaders were imprisoned or forced into exile.

The "petit Vuillaumot" as the Norman peasants had nick-named him, who often entertained him in his childhood, was more popular than ever. He raised to the ground the stone castles of his vassals, and could rule undivided the whole of Normandy of which he was now the undisputed Duke.

October 1047. The Truce of God

The Battle of Val-es-dunes over, Guillaume brought order to his dominion with the help of the Church.

At the Church of Sainte-Paix in Caen he summoned a convocation of Norman Bishops and Seigneurs.

The Truce of God was proclaimed which defined the terms of warfare :
- no warfare was permitted during Advent and Lent nor between Ascension and Whitsun,
- no fighting was allowed at weekends.

The Norman Lords, took oath over the relics of Saint Ouen and agreed to respect the "Duke's Peace". Disobedience incurred banishment and excommunication and the seizure of all their possessions.

Subsequent to the Council of Peace, around 1050 AD, William decided to make the town of Caen the nerve centre of his political operations by having a castle built there.

Part of the Caen castle ramparts as they can be seen today.

Conflict with the King of France

1052. The Siege of Arques

William of Arques, William's uncle, took advantage of his nephew's departure to the Cotentin to proclaim himself Duke of Normandy.

This was too much ; William's fury at its height, he took another ride across Normandy and laid siege to the castle at Arques where his perjured uncle had taken refuge, supported by the King of France.

After several weeks of siege the hungry soldiers of William of Arques came out of the castle, but the Duke of Normandy knew how to be generous : he saved their lives and that of their chief.

11th Century spur

Iron pincers of 11th Century

11th Century Bridle-bits

11th Century Army insignia

1054. The Battle of Mortemer-en-Bray

Henry I of France irritated and above all frightened by the growing power of William, formed an alliance with the latter's enemies : Geoffrey Martel, Count of Anjou and the Counts of Chartres and Poitou. In order to annex Norman territory, a formidable army was assembled. Split in two to form a pincer movement : the western force commanded by the King of France advanced on the centre of the Duchy via Mantes and Évreux ; the other in the north-east under Prince Eude, the King's brother, through the Beauvais Country crossed the Ducal Marshes towards Aumale in the direction of Rouen.

William therefore put in a force on each front, heading one himself against Henry I. His half-brother Robert of Mortain commanded the other, with the Counts Cauchois and Brayon, allowing the French to advance to Mortemer-en-Bray. Easy movement through affluent countryside with relaxed discipline favoured pillage. The Normans put in a surprise attack on the French at dawn ; it was a massacre.

Informed by a runner, William sent news of his misfortune to the King of France by Raoul de Toeni, who, perched in an oak tree, proclaimed the news to the French camp. On hearing tidings of the defeat and flight of his brother, Henry I struck camp and left Normandy.

Horse-shoes and nails of 11th Century

11th Century arrow-heads

Photos : Patrick David, Musée de Normandie

Monument in the middle of the Varaville marshes at the spot where the battle took place

Right : photo illustrates terrain and marshes around Varaville

8

1057. The Battle of Varaville

henry I formed a new alliance with Geoffrey Martel, Count of Anjou. His dream was to appropriate the Norman Lands and rid himself of an embarrassing vassal. They invaded southern Normandy burning and pillaging as they went. After taking Caen, they followed the Roman road.

William was unruffled : he could count on his People. He made no attempt to stop the French and Angevins advancing on to the bridge across the Dives.

Lying low, with his men in the Bavent woods he knew that with the incoming tide, the Dives would flood the marshes and the little wooden bridge would not support the heavy wagons loaded with booty.

Everything happened as he had foreseen. The French soldiers, taken unawares by the rising tide and harassed by William's peasants behind them were drowned.

The King of France never got over it : it was said he died of shame a few years later.

In 1049, the Duke of Normandy was twenty-two. Having put down the revolts in the Duchy and found sure allies in the Church his thoughts turned to founding a family. He must find a wife befitting the great lord he now was and who would bear him numerous offspring.

His choice fell on Matilda, daughter of the Count of Flanders "very comely of person and generous of heart" in the words of William of Jumieges, chronicler of the time.

It was a political choice too, that gave the Duke of Normandy the benevolent neutrality of his powerful neighbour of Flanders.

The Pope, however, opposed the union : William and Matilda had a common ancestor, Rollo the founder of Normandy; they were therefore cousins at fifth remove. Leo IX at the Roman Synod, at which all the Norman Bishops were present, forbade the marriage, on pain of excommunication.

Lanfranc it was, Prior of the Abbey of Bec Hellouin, the Duke's faithful counsellor and friend who went to Rome to plead his cause.

The Pope finally allowed the Wedding on condition of the building of two abbeys in Caen : one for men (Saint-Etienne) consecrated by Lanfranc in 1077, the other for ladies (La Trinité) consecrated in 1066.

Portraits of William and Matilda. *Arch. Calv. Series F*

"How William the King, having brought Peace to the Land, was minded to found an abbey", such was the way the Norman chroniclers chose to depict their sovereign, so appreciated for his support of the Church and public order. The two abbeys founded by William and his wife Matilda, respectively. Saint Etienne and La Trinité are the finest buildings in Caen. *Bib. mun. de Rouen ms Y 26 fol. 101, photo Didier Tragin - Catherine Lancien*

Above : The abbaye aux Dames in Caen
Right : The abbaye aux Hommes consecrated by Lanfranc in 1077

England in William's time

England, successively invaded by the Saxons and the Angles, had not been pacified as had Normandy after its foundation in 911.

It was a country ravaged by Danish raids for the one part and divided by internal rivalries on the other.

Not before the coming of Alfred King of Wessex (871-901) did the Country begin to find some stability though not really before the year 1000.

His heirs had neither the foresight nor the force needed. Ethelred the Unready unable to withstand a more massive Danish invasion than ever, fled to Normandy, taking his sons, Elfred and Edward to his brother-in-law Richard II, Duke of Normandy.

Peace came at last and Edward was crowned King of England in 1043. He was never to forget the welcome he had received from his Uncle, Duke Richard, nor the help from Robert the Magnificient with an attempted landing. He was to maintain too his affection for his nephew William of Normandy.

King Edward, good and virtuous, known as Edward the Confessor, had no children, for which reason he envisaged William, of Viking blood like himself, as heir to the throne of England.

Above left : Coin of Edward the Confessor

King Edward sends Harold on a Mission

Musée de la Tapisserie de Bayeux

The Oath and Perjury of Harold

In 1064, the aged King Edward feeling his end was near, charged his brother-in-law Harold with a mission : to go to Normandy, meet William and announce his decision to make him his heir.
Harold, buffeted by adverse winds, landed in Picardy. Taken prisoner by Guy of Ponthieu, he was taken to the Norman Duke in return for a ransom.
William was cunning ; he decided to put Harold, whom he distrusted, to the test. He took him to Brittany to fight against Duke Conan who had pretentions to Norman territory. In appreciation of Harold's prowess William dubbed him knight on the field of battle.
On his return to Court, William carefully arranged for Harold to take an oath. In the presence of all the Norman dignitaries he made him swear on the Gospel, fidelity and obedience.
Harold did not see, under the cloth of gold on which rested the sacred book, the relics that William had placed there.

"When Harold raised his hand to swear, that hand trembled and the flesh quivered but he had sworn and promised".

This scene is vital. William knew precisely the importance for the Church and all his people the weight of such an oath. He allowed Harold to depart, sure from then on, of his royal destiny.

Shortly after Harold's return to the English Court, Edward died. He was hardly in his grave when Harold was proclaimed King of England, on 6th January 1066.
The Saxons urged the powerful Count of Wessex to take the throne. Harold had friends at Court in the person of his sister, Edward's own wife and he was greatly popular throughout the Country generally.

Harold takes an oath to William over two reliquaries

Musée de la Tapisserie de Bayeux

Diplomatic Preparations

With news of Harold's treason William decided to undertake the reconquest of what he considered to be his rightful heritage.

The months that followed Harold's rise to power was to be a time of intense activity diplomatically, for William to obtain military aid or, short of this, benevolent neutrality.

• Concerning the Papacy :

William sent emissaries to Rome. He wished to see Harold punished for his perjury, an act aggravated by his coronation by Stigand, a bishop lately excommunicated by the Pope for having unlawfully become Archbishop of Canterbury.

The Pope, convinced by the case put before him, gave his assent to the reconquest ; and what is more, he entrusted William with the "Vexillium Sancti Pietri" (The Standard of Saint Peter : a white flag with a cross of gold that the Bayeux Tapestry shows the Duke of Normandy flying proudly). Thus, virtually with the Pope's blessing the Norman expedition took on the character of a holy war, seen as a crusade against the usurper.

• Concerning his neighbours :

William obtained the discreet support of the Holy Roman Emperor, as well as the backing of his brother-in-law the Count of Flanders.
Where the King of France was concerned, he could count on his neutrality during the conflict.

• Concerning Norway :

Its King, Harald Hardrada, who had always had designs on England, envisaged a second front on the north-east of the Country with the help of Tostig, Harold's brother, lately taken to piracy on the high seas.

Carpenters fell trees and build boats

Military Preparations

William, not without difficulty, managed to convince his barons of the rightness of his expedition against the usurper Harold. He could however, count on their troops. As time passed, enthusiasm spread over the Norman frontiers and more than 15 000 soldiers, Normans, Bretons, Angevins, Flemmings, Picards, Poitevins, and even Normans from Sicily prepared for the invasion of England.

Building the Fleet

For six months naval workshops were set up all along the Norman coast line, mainly near the forests of Bonneville-sur-Touques and Bavent where the boat-builders used freshly-cut timber. It was floated down to the workshops at Dives and Sallenelles.

It is estimated that over 500 vessels were built. William also requisitioned fishing boats from as far away as Aquitaine. The finest ship, the Mora, was given by the Duchess Matilda to her husband and contained up to 600 men.

Other relatives were not slow to act : Odo his half-brother contributed 100 ships and his other half-brother, the Count of Mortain sent 120. These ships were equipped to carry provisions, soldiers and all the cavalry. No single detail of the loading of arms and animals has been forgotten in the Bayeux Tapestry.

During the preparations that lasted several months, the Norman Duke divided his time between Troarn Abbey close by the tidal waters of the Dives, where he could keep an eye on the construction of his fleet based at the town of Dives and at his home in Bonneville.

Troarn Abbey

Remains of the Chateau at Bonneville-sur-Touques

Before his Departure

William solemnly appointed Matilda as Regent of Normandy for the whole period that the expedition would take. On 18th June 1066 in the presence of the highest dignitaries of the Duchy, both were present at the consecration of the abbaye aux Dames in Caen, offering their daughter, Cecile, whom they richly endowed, to be brought up in the Abbey.

Musée de la Tapisserie de Bayeux

The Conquest

The Crossing

The entire fleet was concentrated in the Dives Estuary, waiting impatiently for favourable winds and the orders of their Chief, Duke William.

Finally on 10th September 1066 "a forest of masts", with ships taking 12 to 15 000 men, 3 000 horses, arms and provisions put out to sea. When a storm broke out the ships were forced to put back to Saint-Valery-sur-Somme in Northern France. After three weeks of waiting on the Picardy coast for fair winds the Fleet again set sail. This time it landed at Pevensey on the South coast of England on 29th September 1066.

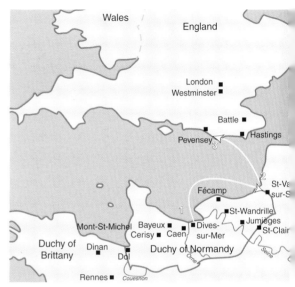

1) William embarked with his fleet from Dives-sur-Mer, 10th September 106
2) The storm forced the vessels to put back to Saint-Valery-sur-Somme
3) Landing at Pevensey on 29th September

omté
Flandre

Above : Aerial View and Below : Beach and Mouth of the Dives where Duke William assembled the fleet that took his mighty army over to the English coast. These two scenes from the Bayeux Tapestry Museum illustrate the Conquest of England.

The Conquest of England

The Battle of York-25th September 1066

W hilst William's fleet was getting ready to land, King Harold had to face another invasion, this time in the north of the Country.

A Norwegian force led by Harald Hardrada, soon joined by troops led by Tostig, Harold's brother in rebellion against him, landed on 18th September in the Humber Estuary.

Two days later they advanced on York. They did not count on Harold's determination : he raised an army against the Viking invaders. At the Battle of Stamford Bridge Harald Hardrada and Tostig were killed and Harold allowed the few survivors to get away.

The Battle of Hastings-14th October 1066

S carcely had Harold recovered from his striking victory over the Norwegians when he learnt of the Norman landing at Pevensey. He had a presentiment that this would be a stiffer fight. He remembered the oath William had made him make. He was told that William had built defence-works at Pevensey and intended going to London to take power. Harold therefore marched his troops south to cut off the Norman army. He needed about ten days to reach the place occupied by the French who had camped on the night of 13th October at the foot of Battle Hill not far from Hastings.

Harold hoped to surprise them the following morning. William was quicker : he moved first to attack.

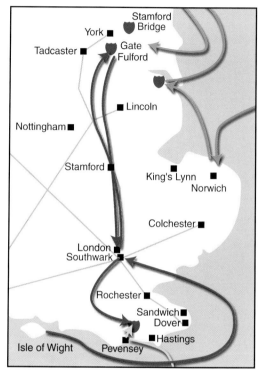

—— Harold	—— Harald
········ William	∿∿∿∿ Roman road
—— Tostig	⬟ Battles of 1066

Ruins of Hastings Castle - *Photo Annie Fettu*

Positions at the start

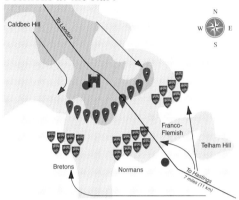

Positions at mi-day

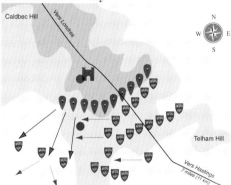

Final Positions

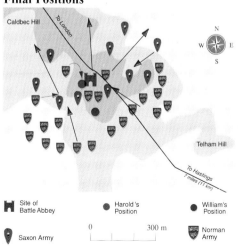

H Site of Battle Abbey

Harold's Position

William's Position

Saxon Army

Norman Army

0   300 m

William's tactics

With carefully planned tactics the Normans took the central position of the Battle-line; the French and Flemish were to the north-east, headed by Robert de Beaumont, the Bretons commanded by Alan of Brittany occupied the front to the west.

The archers were to the fore, estimated at a thousand, then came the infantry armed with pikes and javelins and bringing up the rear were over two thousand horsemen.

The Battle-line, below the hill and in marshland was some 800 metres wide.

Opposite the French, positioned on the top of Battle hill were the Saxons, in greater numbers but consisting solely of the Fyrd* and the Housecarles*.

*The Fyrd : peasants required to fight for their feudal lord.

*Housecarles : Elite royal bodyguard armed with shields and battle-axes.

Battle Abbey - *Photo Philippe Pique*

Hastings or the reasons for Victory

The Mora, a ship given by Matilda, that flew the Papal flag

The Saxons when the day of battle dawned were well placed :
- they knew the terrain,
- they had returned victorious from their battle near York against the Norwegians,
- they stood in serried ranks, shield to shield, not leaving even a chink to be pierced by a stone or a French arrow,
- they were 700 metres above the enemy lines below, on the edge of the marshes.

However, little by little the tide turned in favour of the French. Carried away by over confidence, they risked leaving their vantage point to pursue the Bretons into the marshes. William was quick to see his advantage of this breach in the Saxon lines. He brought in the Norman horsemen, shortly joined by the Breton horsemen who had fled but whom Bishop Odo brought back into action inflicting heavy casualties on the enemy camp.

Harold was mortally wounded by an arrow in his eye ; his two brothers also died.

By the evening of the day of battle, desolation reigned in the Saxon Camp from which the survivors had fled.

It can be seen in retrospect that the Saxons were behind-hand in warfare. They had no cavalry and were not equipped with coats of mail. With tactics based on fighting from a fixed position, movement proved fatal.

Ruins of Hastings Castle - *Photo Annie Fettu*

The Battle of Hastings

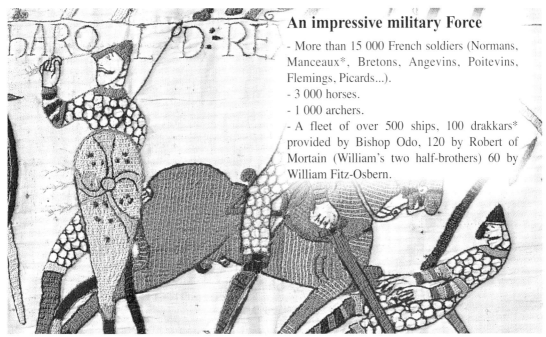

An impressive military Force

- More than 15 000 French soldiers (Normans, Manceaux*, Bretons, Angevins, Poitevins, Flemings, Picards...).
- 3 000 horses.
- 1 000 archers.
- A fleet of over 500 ships, 100 drakkars* provided by Bishop Odo, 120 by Robert of Mortain (William's two half-brothers) 60 by William Fitz-Osbern.

William raises his helmet so that men recognise him *Musée de la Tapisserie de Bayeux*

Harold struck in the eye by the fatal arrow *Musée de la Tapisserie de Bayeux*

* Manceaux : from the County of Maine
* Viking ships

The Companions of William at the Battle of Hastings
Archives départementales du Calvados - Photo Pascal Sellin

22

William, King of England

The Coronation of William

William, known henceforth as William the Conqueror, having shown his military superiority, set off on his march to London, the Capital : a long march, punctuated by pillage and burning in the guise of reprisals against the Saxon population. His route took him through Romney Dover and Canterbury.

His last fight was on the bridge across the Thames which finally left him in charge of the city on fire. He chose Christmas Day to be crowned at Westminster Abbey by Eldred, Archbishop of York in the presence of all the nobility.

During the coronation total confusion reigned outside the Abbey, since the Norman soldiers, probably fearing a revolt had set fire to houses in the vicinity. William, King of England Duke of Normandy and Maine was now head of a domain quite as powerful as France. His reign was to last for over twenty years.

Lords and castles recorded in the Domesday Book 1086

Power over the whole Country

The following months saw William and those close to him assume power over the whole Country. He appointed those around him, head of shires and counties to the detriment of course of the former Saxon Lords.

He, his wife Matilda and his half-brothers shared between them a quarter of the lands in the Kingdom ; fifteen of the lords close to him were given a third.

When in the Spring of 1067 William returned to Normandy, the people gave him a triumphal welcome. He celebrated Easter in Fécamp as if "his ship had come home".

William, a Ruling Monarch

In his absence from Normandy, the Duke had had the good sense to appoint as Regent his wife Matilda, seconded by his old friend Roger of Beaumont.

The genius of William the Conqueror was to make use of people he could trust and to bring to the lands he ruled stable institutions.

The new king retained the Saxon divisions of the Kingdom into Counties whilst putting men of his own in charge. He looked after finances by creating the Court of the Exchequer, the role of which was to supervise the Sheriffs'* accounts.

He strengthened the Feudal system : every Lord became his vassal, owed his fief and received protection in return for homage : in time of war for example he must raise an army in the service of the Crown.

*Sheriff (Shire-reeve) : a "First Magistrate appointed by the King".

William, King of England

The Domesday Book

In 1086, King William undertook a census of the entire Kingdom, county by county, everything was recorded : lands, men, beasts and buildings. An entire land-survey ahead of its time, this "Book of Judgement Day" gives us a picture of the Feudal System established in England after the Conquest ; it was in essence a vast fiscal operation so that nothing could escape Tax.

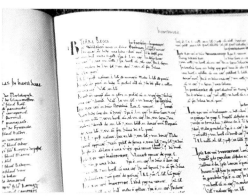

Facsimile of the Domesday Book
Archives départementales du Calvados

William and his Times

William contributed to the development of a style of Anglo-Norman architecture that we can still admire today. Thanks to Caen Stone the quarrying of which grew rapidly from the time of the Conquest, resulting in superb edifices both in England and Normandy. Two of these are Westminster Abbey and the Tower of London.

From the time of William the Conqueror, Normandy experienced a new economic prosperity. The monks of the many abbeys that William had supported, cleared the land, managed forests, grew crops, arranged water-supply and planted vines.

Norman towns developed, Caen especially, due to its quarries, but Falaise too where the Fair of Guibray rivalled the great fairs of Champagne in attracting English traders.

Salt was produced at Isigny, Dives and Touques, making possible the curing of bacon and fish. Finally the "Scriptoria" which were the editorial departments in the abbeys, flourished widely. At Fécamp, as at Saint-Etienne in Caen, they contributed to the growth of intellectual life.

Transport of Caen Stone : a model. *Musée de la Tapisserie de Bayeux*

The Scriptorium.　　　　　　　　*Musée de la Tapisserie de Bayeux*

Norman architecture in England

Battle Abbey

▲
The Great Lodge (1330) was built next to an older gate-house dating from the 11th century.
The Abbey was built to commemorate the Battle of Hastings.
The High Altar marks the exact spot where Harold died

Model of the Tower of London
Musée de la Tapisserie de Bayeux ▶

Model of Winchester Cathedral
Musée de la Tapisserie de Bayeux

Some examples in Normandy itself

Cerisy-la-Forêt Abbey

Church at Thaon

Château de Chambois

Interior of the Church of Saint-Nicolas in Caen

Notre-Dame de Dives-sur-Mer

Ego Willelmus rex anglor princeps normannor & coenomannoru. trado ecclię di. qua psalute mea. uxorif. liberor. parentuq; meor in honore beati stephani cadomi construxi. rotomagi sup sequana. cetariu unu. ita ut liceat monachif ineo quietu habere quicqd uini ut cuicunq; rei adusu monachor. desuo emerint. qd admonasteriu sine uenditione deferre uoluerint. Homini aut uini tantu qui ineodem celario manebit. liceat unoquoq; anno centu modios uini quietos habere. abomib; grediribus & captionibus. data in tantu illa modiatione. que de centu modiis d̄ cabalus ineadem uilla. Quicqd u uini sup centu modios habuerit inter consuetudini reseruau. inmodiatione. ingredi tibus. incaptionibus. Inceterif u uenalib; rebus tam intra aqua qua extra quietu ee eu concedo. sedm quietudiné alior hominu ecclarioqui neadé uilla quietudiné habent. Concedo etia terrá quá hugo de rosel tenuit deme in gainuilla. quá dedit monasterio predicto cu mona chus factus est.

Signū Willi regif angloz comitif normannor
Signū maꝛhildif regine
+Ricardus de corcello
+Gaufridi constantiensis epf
Signū fulconif de almou.

H 1830

William in this Charter, drawn up between 1066 and 1083 cedes to the monks of the abbaye aux Hommes in Caen the use of a wine-cellar in Rouen "for the salvation of his soul". *Archives départementales du Calvados, Photo Pascal Sellin*

William and the Church

William quickly understood the extent to which the church, all powerful in the 11th Century could help him reinforce his own power. He made the acquaintance of an Italian monk, prior of the Abbey of Bec Hellouin : Lanfranc of Pavia. The Duke was soon impressed with his intelligence and his plain-speaking. In 1050 he made him his counsellor. Lanfranc was an able man. He succeeded in getting the Pope to waive the excommunication threatening William, regarding his marriage to his cousin. He became the first Abbot of the abbaye aux Hommes at Caen in 1070, and later Archbishop of Canterbury.

On his advice, William called Convocations (of bishops) to reaffirm Church

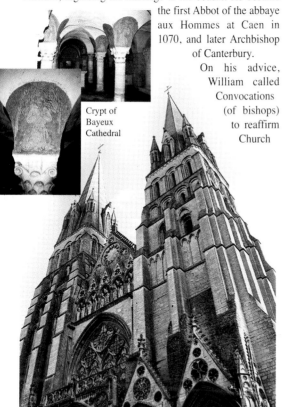

Crypt of Bayeux Cathedral

Cathedral Notre-Dame de Bayeux 11th and 13th centuries

principles : celibate clergy, prohibition of Simony and trade in relics. He re-organised the Church in England, replacing English bishops by Normans. Finally he encouraged the founding of new Benedictine Abbeys following the Cluny reforms : Battle Abbey was one, Lewes another.

William's Tragic End

The conflict with Philip, King of France worsened and, High Treason : William's own son Robert Courteheuse, fled to the Capetian Court.

Wishing to repossess the Vexin William ordered his troops to attack Mantes-la-Jolie which he set on fire. It is said that his horse took fright at the flames and shyed. William who had become stout, became impaled on the pommel of his saddle.

The accident proved fatal ; the Conqueror never recovered. He was taken to Rouen, his Capital city, where he died on the morning of 9th September 1087. His last wish was to be buried in the town he had loved so much : Caen, in the abbaye aux Hommes. It was a way of joining Queen Matilda who, for four years past, reposed in the abbaye aux Dames.

The roads being impassable he was taken by water, the corpse wrapped in an ox-hide to serve as a shroud. Coming up the river Orne the boat was accompanied by a large crowd. On arrival in Caen the monks of the Abbey took charge of the dead king to take him to his last resting place. At the moment his coffin was being lowered into the grave, which was too small, it split open when attempts were made to force it down. The pestilential smell thus exuded forced those present to retire.

At this moment, one named Ascelin appeared and made objection : the land on which the Abbey was built belonged, he claimed, to one, Arthur his father. He opposed the right to continue the funeral. After having received the sum of sixty sous, Ascelin withdrew his objection and the funeral rite continued.

During the Wars of Religion, William's tomb was profaned by the Protestants as was that of Matilda.The bones were dispersed with the exception of a femur, piously buried by the monks in a leaden coffin. In 1742, the Intendant of Caen orderd a vault to be made and covered with a marble slab. The slab was broken during the French Revolution in 1793. Not until 1802 did the Prefet of Calvados have a new plaque put in place. It is this that is seen today by visitors to the Abbey.

Epilogue

The Abbey Church dedicated to the Holy Trinity

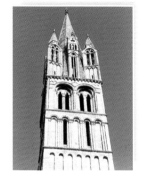

The Abbey Church of Saint-Etienne

On the death of William the Anglo-Norman Kingdom was split up. His eldest son Robert was heir to Normandy and William Rufus was crowned King of England.

Robert Courteheuse, very much the knight, took part in the Crusades with Godrey de Bouillon and fought with valour at Jerusalem. He returned in 1100 to hear of the death of William Rufus whilst hunting in the New Forest and that his younger brother Henry Beauclerc had taken the English throne. The latter scheming and ambitious, dreamed of ruling both Normandy and England.

At the Battle of Tinchebray in 1106, Duke Robert was taken prisoner by Henry's soldiers and Beauclerc reigned over the Anglo-Norman Kingdom as Henry I.

In 1204 after Philip-Auguste took Chateau Gaillard, Normandy became French after the Anglo-Norman phase of nearly 150 years.

The nave of the Abbey Church of Holy Trinity in Norman style architecture

The Norman nave of the Abbey Church of Saint-Etienne

WILLIAM'S EPITAPH

HERE LIES
THE INVINCIBLE WILLIAM THE CONQUEROR
NORMAN DUKE AND ENGLISH KING
FOUNDER OF THIS HOUSE
WHO DIED IN THE YEAR 1087

QUEEN MATILDA'S EPITAPH

BENEATH THIS SLAB IN THIS TOMB SUPERB
AND IN HER HONOUR
LIES MATILDA, MIRROR OF ALL VIRTUES
OF BLOOD ROYAL SHE HAD AS FATHER
THE DUKE OF FLANDERS WHILST HER MOTHER ADÈLE
WAS THE DAUGHTER OF ROBERT KING OF FRANCE
AND SISTER OF HENRY, A MONARCH TOO

JOINED IN MARRIAGE TO THE NOBLE KING WILLIAM
SHE RAISED UP THIS SAME MONASTERY
AND THIS VERY CHURCH, ENDOWING THE FORMER
WITH LANDS AND ALL GOODS AND CHATTELS
AND BY HER FAVOUR THE LATTER WAS CONSECRATED

FULL OF PITY FOR THE POOR
SPURRED ON BY ARDENT PIETY
COUNTLESS TREASURE DID SHE GIVE
SO LITTLE FOR HER, YET SO GREAT FOR THE NEEDY
THUS WAS SHE NUMBERED WUTH THE ELECT
WHO REJOICE IN HEAVEN AND LIFE ETÈRNAL
ON FIRST NOVEMBER AFTER PRIME

- 1083 -

A Slab in black Tournai Marble marks the tomb of Queen Matilda

The tomb of William the Conqueror before the High Altar

Right-hand page : the Church in Thaon 11th Century

ISBN 978-2-912925-22-0

5 €

THE TIMES
SECOND TOURNAMENT OF THE MIND

500 **NEW**
BRAIN TEASERS
FROM MENSA

LOGIC   You have brown, blue, black and green socks in your drawer in the ratio of 2 to 3, to 4, to 5 pairs. How many socks must you take out to be sure of having a pair?

DIAGRAMMATIC   In the diagram the planet orbits the sun once every 5 years. The asteroid has entered an orbit which intersects that of the planet and takes 26 years to complete its orbit. If the asteroid is 27.69231 degrees away from the intersection point, when, if ever, will it collide with the planet?

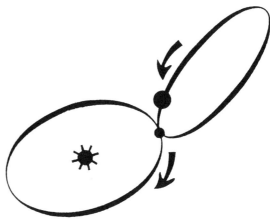

VERBAL You have to place two letters in the brackets so that they finish the word on the left and begin the word on the right. When you read the letters in the brackets downwards you will find a new word. Can you tell us what this word is?

DOG   ( )   TINS
FORE   ( )   ARE
TELL   ( )   MINE

MATHS A tramp collects cigarette ends from which he makes full cigarettes. He has amassed 100 ends. He knows that he can make one full cigarette from four ends. How many full cigarettes can he make and smoke altogether?

MISCELLANEOUS A long-distance tanker has developed a leak. It travels at a speed of 90 mph, leaving a trail of petrol behind it which ignited at the moment the tanker set off. The flames follow the tanker at a speed of 89.5 mph. The tanker stops after 500 miles. How long will it be, to the nearest second, before it explodes, assuming that it does explode?

WORKINGS

TRIVIA

1 Name the race of wild creatures who, in Greek mythology, were half-human and half-horse.

2 What is the common name of the large, flightless, long-legged Australian bird which can be up to 150 cm tall and 45 kg in weight, and which has dark-brown, hairlike plumage?

3 Name the card game in which the winner is determined by the amount of 'tricks', and in which the gameplay centres around the 'trump' card.

4 What is the common name of a certain plant of the mustard family, whose sharp-tasting leaves are often used in salads, and which is believed to be native to Western Asia?

5 Name the Spanish artist, born in Malaga, who painted 'Guernica'.

ANSWERS

LOGIC   Nary's corner shop was losing some business to the new supermarket so she ran a 'Guess the amount of Jelly Beans in the Jar' competition. It was a very small jar indeed. Ann guessed 43 beans, Bett guessed 34 beans, Charles guessed 41 beans. One of them was off by six beans, another by three beans and another by only one. How many beans were really there?

DIAGRAMMATIC   Here is a diagram of a flattened cube. Can you reconstruct it and tell us which of the completed cubes cannot be made?

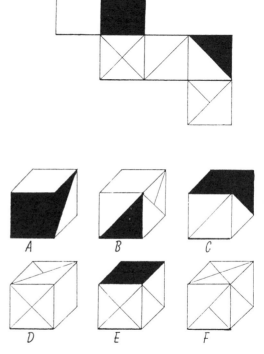

VERBAL Which three-lettered word can be placed before the following words to create four new words? Here are the words:

BUCKLE   GET   SNIP

MATHS A train maintains an average speed of 140 mph from station A to station B. It then returns from B to A over exactly the same distance at an average speed of 56 mph. What was the average speed for the whole journey?

MISCELLANEOUS Look at the diagram of the signpost and, by working out the logic, find the distance to London.

WORKINGS

TRIVIA

1 What is the name of the British naturalist, born in 1809, who originated the concept that living things evolve by natural selection?

2 Name the Swedish tennis player, born in 1956, who was the world's leading tennis player in the late 1970s, and who won the men's singles at Wimbledon for five consecutive years.

3 Name the spa town in West Central England famous for its public school and annual drama and music festival.

4 What is the name of the temple on the hill of the Acropolis in Athens, dedicated to the goddess Athena?

5 Name the mental disorder associated with a breakdown of the thinking processes and isolation from reality, considered by some psychologists to be the worst of the mental disorders.

ANSWERS

LOGIC   How can you arrange seven matches so that they equal 200?

DIAGRAMMATIC   The diagram is a strange dartboard. Using three darts at a time, you must discover how many different ways there are of scoring a total of 108. Once you have used a combination of numbers, you cannot use it again in a different order. All darts must score.

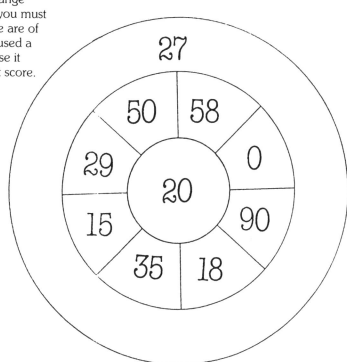

VERBAL   Can you replace the first letter of each of the words either side of the brackets with another letter so that a new word is formed? When you read the new letters together, they form a different word.

CARE	( )	FADE
MICE	( )	DEAL
STEM	( )	FLEX
GRANGE	( )	DOZE
EAT	( )	SLUMP
MEAT	( )	WAKE
WARN	( )	BLAND

MATHS   Your clock is correct at midnight but gains 3 minutes per hour. You look at the clock and see that it shows 5.15 am. You know that the clock had stopped exactly 1 hour ago. What is the correct time now?

MISCELLANEOUS   During a cricket match, Andy scores 38 runs more than Bill. Bill, on the other hand, scores 37 runs fewer than Chris. Eric scores 17 runs more than Dave, and Chris scores 18 more than Eric. The total runs scored by Bill and Eric is 63. What is the total number of runs scored by these five players during the match?

WORKINGS

TRIVIA

1 Name the French artist whose growth was stunted by a childhood accident, and specialized in a technique known as 'lithography'.

2 What is the name of the Continental cycling race founded in 1903 and consisting of some twenty stages?

3 Name the famous town on the extreme western point of England, lying at a distance of 970 km from the equally well-known town at the northern tip of Scotland.

4 Name the German Nazi politician, born in 1897, who entered the Reichstag in 1928 when he was appointed Minister of Propaganda.

5 What is the name of the temperature scale using the freezing point of water as zero and the boiling point as 100 degrees, now officially called Celsius?

ANSWERS

LOGIC   A boat is battling against a stream to safety. It is 15 miles from an island. It is travelling at 8 mph but the rate of flow from the stream is 2 mph against the ship. The ship uses 10 gallons of fuel every hour and has a tank capacity of 14 gallons. Will it reach safety?

DIAGRAMMATIC   Here is a strange signpost. Look at the diagram and, by working out the logic, fill in the missing distance to Cairo. Vowels have a value each, as do consonants.

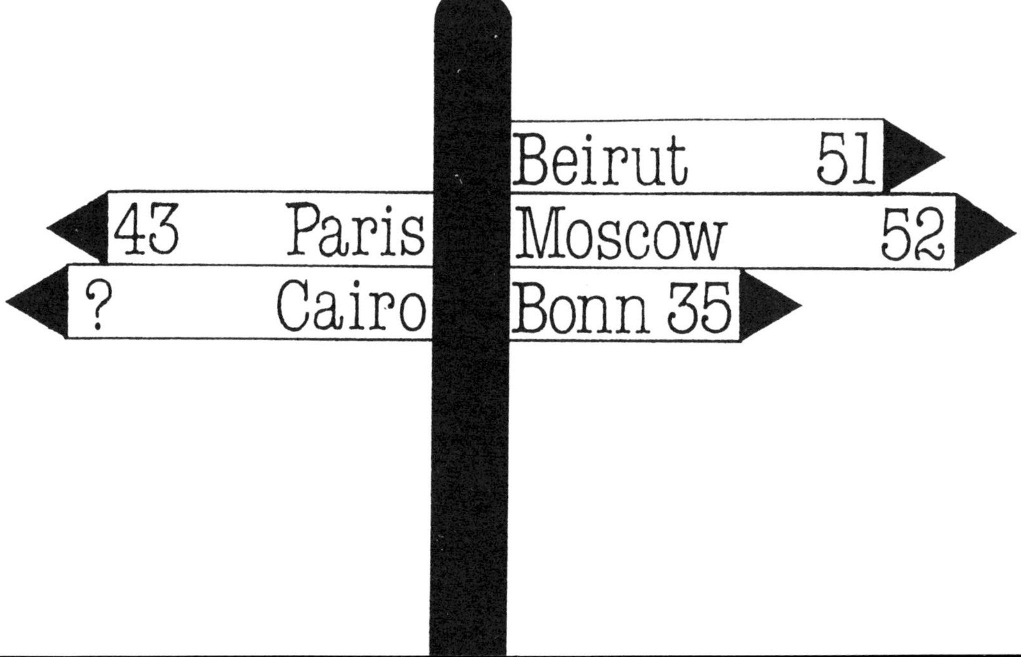

Beirut 51

43 Paris — Moscow 52

? Cairo — Bonn 35

VERBAL   We have arranged the word *DEPTH* so that it reads the same downwards as well as across. The intention is to complete the square so that it reads four more words across and down. The first will begin with the letter E of *DEPTH*, the second with the P and so on. Can you tell us what word begins with the letter E? Here are all the letters which you must use to complete the square.

E E E E E E I I I

D D R R S M M

```
D E P T H
E
P
T
H
```

MATHS   You have a total of £32.13 but it is all in 2p, 5p and 10p coins. You know that you have an equal amount of each coin. How many coins are there in total?

MISCELLANEOUS   A rich man decided that he would give every male in a town of 10,000 people £50 and to every female he offered £45. Only a certain fraction of the male population claimed the money and only a ninth of the females collected their dues. If he gave away a total of £50,000, what fraction of the males collected their dues?

WORKINGS

TRIVIA

1 Name the British sculptor, born in Yorkshire in 1898, whose sculptures develop the 'Mother and Child' theme.

2 What is the name of the lowest temperature than can theoretically be attained, equal to −273.15 degrees Centigrade?

3 What is the name of the religion of some 9 million Indians, founded in the 19th century and combining Hindu and Islamic ideas?

4 Give the general name of the theories and practices based on a belief in hidden supernatural forces that supposedly explain phenomena that science cannot.

5 What is the scientific name of a condition of the skin, often associated with eczema, in which inflammation and a scaly rash can occur?

ANSWERS

LOGIC In one day of foraging, a tramp has collected 489 cigarette ends. He knows from experience that he can make one full cigarette from nine ends. How many cigarettes can he make in total?

DIAGRAMMATIC Two planets are in orbit around a sun with which they now form a straight line. Both orbit in a clockwise direction and the outer one takes 19 years to complete an orbit. The inner planet takes 8 years to complete an orbit. When will they next form a straight line with each other and the sun?

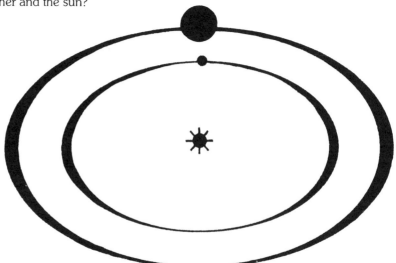

VERBAL Can you replace the first letter of each of the words either side of the brackets with another letter so that a new word is formed? When you read the new letters together you will find that they form another, somewhat hurried, word.

MOUSE   ( )   CARP

GROUND ( )   BERATE

CHEER   ( )   CORE

CHIN   ( )   GRIP

FIELD   ( )   BELL

MATHS A car travels at a speed of 35 mph. Its fuel consumption is 25 miles to the gallon. It has a 10-gallon tank which was full when it started but at that moment began to leak. After 100 miles, the car stops with a completely empty tank. How many gallons per hour was it losing?

MISCELLANEOUS In the jungle there are some rather peculiar insects. Some have two wings, some have four, some have six and some have eight wings. You have just counted 380 wings, which came from an equal number of insects of each kind. How many insects of each type have you discovered?

WORKINGS

TRIVIA

1 Name the musical instrument of the violin family whose greatest 20th-century exponent has been Pablo Casals.

2 What is the name of the fabulous bird associated with sun-worship and representing resurrection and immortality?

3 Name the Russian composer, born in 1873, credited with the composition of a piano concerto called 'Rhapsody on a Theme of Paganini'.

4 What is the name of those sound frequencies which are too high to be audible to the human ear?

5 Name the famous US actor, born in Italy, whose roles in early silent films such as *The Sheik* and *Blood and Sand* established him as the leading idol of the 1920s.

ANSWERS

LOGIC   A small private bus has five seats upstairs and five down. Mrs Black is sitting behind Mr Green, while Mr Roberts is sitting in the front of the bus in front of Mr Smith. Mrs White is seated on the upper deck at the rear and in front of her sits Mr Brown. Mr Jones is also seated on the upper level in a position which places him ahead of Mr Smith. Mrs Taylor is seated upstairs in front of Mrs Peters, who is sitting above Mr Green. Assuming that all the seats are occupied and that the last passenger is Mrs Grey, where is she sitting?

DIAGRAMMATIC   In the diagram each of the symbols has been given a value. You have to find the values and then discover what should replace the question mark.

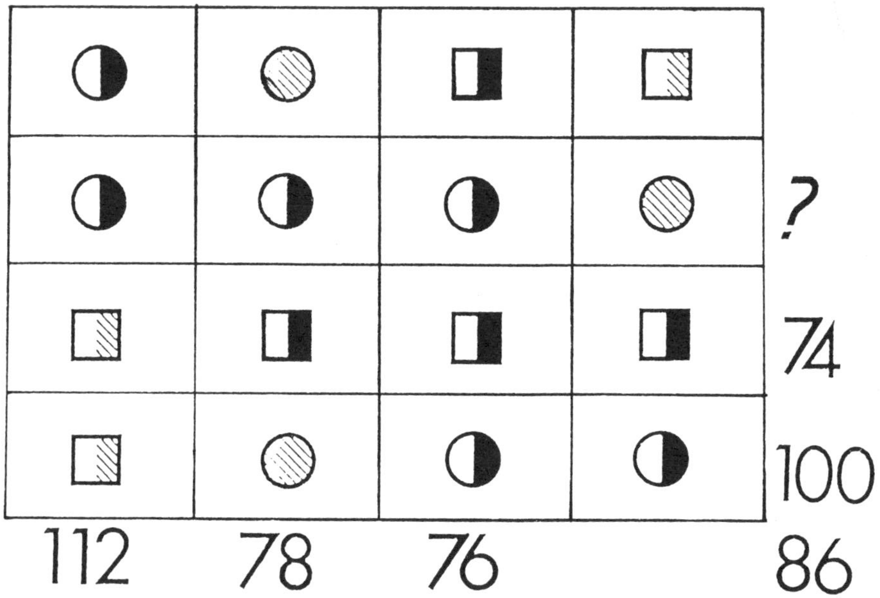

				?
				74
				100
112	78	76		86

VERBAL   Can you find a three-letter word which will go after these letters to form three different words?

CUR   RI   PRI

MATHS   A man set out to walk from one town to another. On the first day, he covered one-half of the total distance. On the second day, he covered one-quarter of the remaining distance and on the third day one-third of what was then left. On the fourth day, he covered one-half and is still 57.25 miles away from his destination. How many miles has he covered so far?

MISCELLANEOUS   A farmer earned a certain sum last week by selling eggs. Brown eggs cost twice as much as white eggs, but of the 112 eggs sold, only 25 per cent were brown. Brown eggs were sold at the price of four for 10p. How much money did the farmer make?

WORKINGS

TRIVIA

1 What is the name of the ancient mixture of spices and gums, burnt for its aroma and employed widely in pagan rituals?

2 Name the style of rock music which incorporates West Indian rhythms and rhythm and blues, and which had a wide popularity in the UK in the early 1970s.

3 What is the name of the game which developed from the children's game of 'Lotto'?

4 Name the biblical brothers whose names became notorious because one of them became 'The world's first murderer' by killing his brother in a fit of jealousy.

5 What is the historical name of the unfree peasants of the Middle Ages who were bound to the soil they tilled?

ANSWERS

LOGIC   You have the misfortune to own an unreliable clock. This one loses exactly 4 minutes every hour. It is now showing 3.30 am and you know that it was correct at midnight, when you set it. You remember that the clock stopped two hours ago. What is the correct time now?

DIAGRAMMATIC   There are several letters here which can be used to spell the word *MITRE*. How many ways can this be done? Each letter is to be regarded as different and, once a combination of letters has been used, it cannot be re-used in a different order. By the way, *TIMER* does *not* spell *MITRE*.

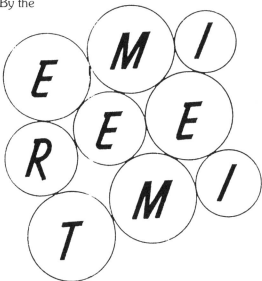

VERBAL You have to place two letters in the brackets so that they finish the word on the left and begin the word on the right. When you read the letters in the brackets downwards you will find a new word. Can you tell us what this word is?

BEG ( ) ROAD
BIN ( ) RENT
BOO ( ) RAP

MATHS A fire engine is on its way to a fire 8 miles away at a speed of 48 mph. It has a tank which holds 100 gallons of water. It has developed a leak, however, and is losing 5 gallons of water per hour. The fire engine will need 99 gallons of water to put out the fire. Will it achieve this?

MISCELLANEOUS In a 200-metre race, Frederick beats William by 25 metres. In order to give William a sporting chance, Frederick starts exactly 28 metres behind the starting line. The race is run again, and both maintain exactly the same speeds. Who wins this time?

WORKINGS

TRIVIA

1 Which of these is known as the 'Father of Comedy'; Aristophanes, Hugo, Shakespeare or Socrates?

2 What is 'musophobia' the fear of?

3 Which of these islands are termed 'The Friendly Islands'; New Hebrides, Seychelles, Fiji or Tonga?

4 How many faces does a dodecahedron have?

5 How else could one describe someone who is said to be 'sedulous'?

ANSWERS

LOGIC Here is a series of letters. You have to work out what they are and then give us the next letter to continue the series.

N E O U I I E?

DIAGRAMMATIC In the 5 × 5 square you will see that three letters have been filled in. It is your task to complete the square with letters in such a way that no two identical letters appear in the same line either horizontally, vertically or diagonally, and that includes the short diagonals of two, three or four squares. The word you must use is *SPACE*.

				S
	P			
			A	

VERBAL The following words are made up of two words which have been merged together. You have to 'un-merge' them and give us the pairs of words.

AEFURRIOCAPE

PRAROIMES

CLOANDRODIFNF

MATHS A cricketer's average in his first 29 innings was 18 runs. After a further 10 innings his average had decreased to 16 runs. What was his average for the last ten innings only?

MISCELLANEOUS What comes next in the second series of letters so that it matches up with the first series?

A D J K N
B E G I ?

WORKINGS

TRIVIA

1 For what was John Nevil Maskelyne famous?

2 For what sport is the Prix de l'Arc de Triomphe trophy awarded?

3 Which horse won the Grand National in 1971?

4 What was the ancient Latin name for Ireland?

5 What is cicim?

ANSWERS

9th | Round

LOGIC In a pools syndicate which successfully won £1347 there were more than two people but less than 100. Each winner was paid in full (pounds only). How many were in the syndicate and how much did each win?

DIAGRAMMATIC In the diagram we know that the top and bottom scales balance perfectly. You have to tell us how many small clubs are needed to balance the bottom set.

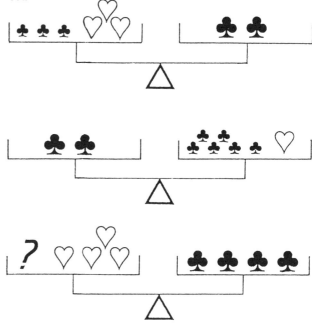

VERBAL The following somewhat cynical comment has had all the vowels replaced and the remaining letters broken up into groups of four. Replace the vowels and solve the comment.

CMMT TSGR PTHT KPSM NTSB TWST SHRS

MATHS A man cashed a cheque at a bank and discovered that the bank cashier had transposed the pounds for pence and the pence for pounds on the cheque, thus giving him far more money. He bought goods for £8.24 and discovered that he now had exactly six times the value of the original cheque. What was the value of the original cheque?

MISCELLANEOUS It takes a hot tap 19 minutes to fill a bath, while it takes the cold tap 24 minutes. The plug has accidentally been left out, however, and the bath will empty itself in 30 minutes. If both taps are left on full, how long, if ever, will it take to fill the bath?

WORKINGS

TRIVIA

1 For what is the 'Dewey-decimal' system used?

2 What is the slang name given to a boxer who leads with his right hand?

3 How many characters are there in the Russian alphabet?

4 By whom was the frozen-food process invented?

5 From which animal does mohair come?

ANSWERS

LOGIC   Two cars are travelling from Birmingham to London. The first car travels from Birmingham at 121 mph while the second travels from London at 120 mph. If the second car leaves 5½ minutes before the first car, which car will be furthest from London when they meet?

DIAGRAMMATIC   In the diagram how many different ways can be found by following the arrows to get from A to B?

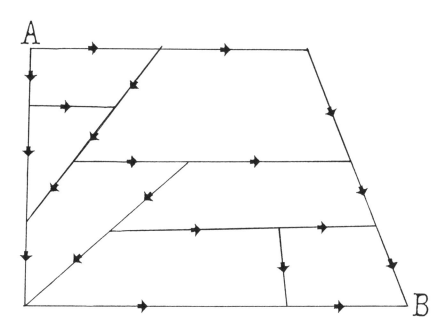

VERBAL   Eight words have been merged together here. However, the letters are in the correct order. You have to 'un-merge' them to find the original words.

CLOCRUOWDDSS
HFOEPARE
DLIEVAED
ROROOASSTTSS

MATHS   A train is travelling at a speed of 48 mph and is 220 yards long. It enters a tunnel which is 2 miles long. How long will it take the whole of the train to pass through the tunnel?

MISCELLANEOUS   If D is worth 1000, E is worth 5, O is worth 2 and Y is worth 20, what is X worth?

WORKINGS

TRIVIA

1 Name the Greek dramatist, born in 496 BC, who wrote 123 plays of which only seven now survive.

2 What is the word describing those who believe that all we know about the world today suggests that the notion of 'God' is a false one?

3 What is the stage name of Robert Allen Zimmerman, born in 1941, a US singer, songwriter and lyricist?

4 Name the processes, discovered by Thomas Graham, for separating mixtures of fluids by diffusion through a semi-permeable membrane.

5 What was the popular phrase used to describe the group of young novelists and dramatists of the 1950s, whose attitudes included dissatisfaction with post-war British society and disrespect for 'The Establishment'?

ANSWERS

LOGIC At a certain golf club it has been discovered that under 100 new untried members played the fifth hole and each has managed to complete it in the same number of strokes. There were over 80 players and the total number of all their strokes came to 1598. They must be novices! What was the number of strokes taken by each of the players on this hole and how many players were there?

DIAGRAMMATIC Here are some numbers:

1 1 2 2 3 3 3 3 3 3 4 4 4 4 4 4 5 5 5 5 6 6 8 8

Place them in the grid in such a way that each segment of three numbers totals 12 and each of the three circles of numbers total 32.

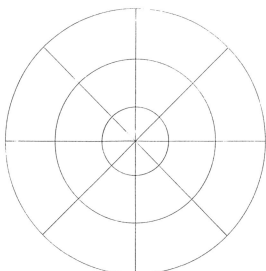

VERBAL   Change the word *TEAR* to *SOBS* in five moves only. Change one letter with each move and create another English word every time.

MATHS   Replace the brackets and mathematical symbols to the left of the equals sign in this series of numbers so that they equal 100.

19 61 3 = 100

MISCELLANEOUS   Sally likes beer but not wine. She hates lamb but adores mutton. She loves cheese but detests milk. Does she like tea?

WORKINGS

TRIVIA

1 Which writer created the character 'Winnie the Pooh'?

2 What sugar is named after a district in Guyana?

3 Who wrote the *Foundation* series?

4 What nationality was Sigmund Freud by birth?

5 Who wrote the children's story *Jemima Puddleduck*?

ANSWERS

LOGIC In an archery contest there are six contestants who are expected to shoot 58 arrows. However, 18 reserves turn up who also want to shoot at the targets. All contestants now shoot exactly the same number of arrows. How many whole arrows do they each shoot?

DIAGRAMMATIC The letters of the word *LYNX* appear in the grid. You begin at the centre L and move from square to touching square but only upwards, downwards or across. You never move diagonally. As you move you collect the four letters of the word in any order. How many times can this be done by finding different routes from the centre L?

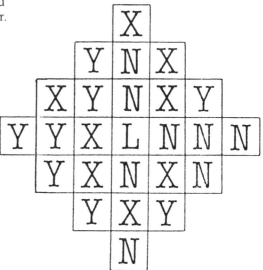

VERBAL In the following list a word appears either side of the brackets. Find the English word which can be placed inside the brackets to make two new words. One will end with the word in the brackets, the other will begin with it. Here are the words:

RIVER ( ) WINDER

MAM ( ) EATEN

NOTE ( ) CASE

MATHS A ship is battling against a current to safety. It is 20 miles from an island. It is travelling at 11 mph but the rate of flow of the current is 2 mph against the ship. The ship uses 13 gallons of fuel every hour and has a tank capacity of 29 gallons. Will it reach safety?

MISCELLANEOUS In a 400-metre race, Fred beats Barry by 24 metres. The race is now run again with Fred starting 27 metres behind the starting line as a handicap. Who wins the race?

WORKINGS

TRIVIA

1 With approximately 10,000 people per square kilometre, which country has the highest population density?

2 In which year did the Dunkirk evacuation take place?

3 Who wrote the novel *Moby Dick*?

4 What is Crêpe Suzette?

5 What is the highest break which can be achieved in snooker?

ANSWERS

LOGIC   Here are the atomic weights of various gases. It seems that a different logic dictates the figures in the list. You must work out the rationale behind the system and find out what the weight of helium should be.

ARGON	102
NEON	78
OXYGEN	126
HELIUM	?

DIAGRAMMATIC   Look at the 16 hexagons in the diagram. In each there are certain objects arranged in a different order. There are some objects repeated more than once in some rectangles. We want you to tell us which pairs of rectangles can be considered identical, since they contain exactly the same objects although perhaps not in the same order.

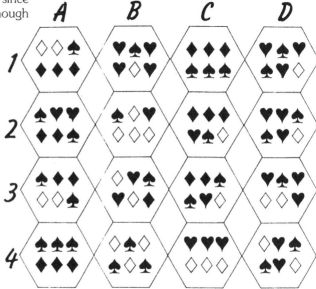

VERBAL   Can you make the names of three composers from this strange sentence by using every letter?

Forlorn diners bleat.

MATHS   A man set out to travel from one town to another. On the first day he covered one-half of the total distance. On the second day he covered one-fifth of the remaining distance. On the third day he covered one-quarter of what was left, and on the fourth day he covered one-third of the rest. He now has 130.8 miles left to go. What distance has he travelled so far?

MISCELLANEOUS   It takes one tap 9 minutes to fill a bath, while it takes the other 27 minutes to fill the bath. The plug has been left out and the bath will empty in 35 minutes. If both taps are left on full, how long, if ever, will it take to fill the bath?

WORKINGS

TRIVIA

1 What major event took place near Naples in AD 74?

2 Which advertising agency is headed by two brothers named Morris and Charles?

3 What is pepsin?

4 At the turn of the century, what was the tallest structure in the world?

5 Which American president's head appears on the one-dollar bill?

ANSWERS

LOGIC   Here are four related series. Can you work out the logic and then give us the next in the series?

A	M	J	J
1:13	13:20	10:23	10:20
M	T	W	T

DIAGRAMMATIC   Start at any corner in the diagram and follow the routes, collecting a total of five numbers which are added together. This includes the corner number. Only one corner can be used per attempt and you cannot retrace your steps. How many different routes are there which total 21?

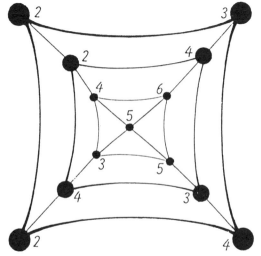

VERBAL Here is another strange sentence. By using every letter you have to find the names of three Far East countries.

No-one bargained in soot.

MATHS A petrol tanker travels at a speed of 80 mph. It is leaking petrol and the petrol catches fire. The petrol flame chases the tanker at a speed of 79 mph. If the tanker stops after 250 miles, when will it explode?

MISCELLANEOUS In a town of 1113 people there lived a rich man. He offered a certain sum to each male and £12 to each female. Of the males, however, only one-sixth claimed the money and of the females only one-quarter claimed their dues. He gave away a total of £3339. How much did he give to each male?

WORKINGS

TRIVIA

1 About what did Euclid write a treatise?

2 What is the name of the motor-racing circuit in Kent just off the A20?

3 Where is the pituitary gland situated?

4 What was the name of Pinocchio's father?

5 Who played the villain in the James Bond film *The Man with the Golden Gun*?

ANSWERS

15th | Round

LOGIC   A boat is sinking. Having struck two icebergs simultaneously, it is in more than a little difficulty. The hole made by the first iceberg will let in enough water to sink the boat in 6 minutes. The hole from the second iceberg is bigger, and would take only 4 minutes to send the boat to its watery grave. Naturally, the pumps are working overtime. In normal circumstances the pumps could empty a hole-less ship in 5 minutes. Well, these aren't normal circumstances and everyone's panicking. When will the boat sink?

DIAGRAMMATIC   In the diagram are the letters of the word *MANDOLINE*. Start at the bottom left-hand corner and move upwards and from left to right, collecting letters as you go. You must finish at the top right-hand corner with nine letters. How many different ways are there of collecting the letters of *MANDOLINE* by this method?

VERBAL Now that you are getting good at finding countries by using every letter of a sentence find three from this one:

I love going into a bar.

MATHS Jimmy didn't like being asked how old he was. Neither did his mother. So she told the enquirer, 'I'm just seven times as old as he is now. In 20 years, he'll be just half my age then.' How old was Jimmy?

MISCELLANEOUS A cricketer's average in his first 10½ innings was 12 runs. After a further 18 innings his average had increased to 45 runs. What was his average for the last 18 innings only?

WORKINGS

TRIVIA

1 Who wrote *The Grapes of Wrath*?

2 Where can Sing-Sing prison be found?

3 Who wrote the poem 'The Jabberwocky', a fantasy story written in half-English?

4 What is special to the Irish about 17 March?

5 Which Greek mythological character performed twelve tasks to free himself from bondage?

ANSWERS

LOGIC   A lorry driver knows that he can average 44 mph with his lorry loaded with bricks. If his lorry is empty he can average 6 mph faster. He left home for the factory at 12 noon. The journey was 25 miles. He stopped off for a cup of tea for a quarter of an hour and was back home a few seconds after 1.15 pm. How many bricks did he leave at the factory?

DIAGRAMMATIC   By starting at the bottom left-hand corner of the diagram and following the arrows to the top right-hand corner, what is the highest score you can attain by adding the numbers together? By the way, each black circle is worth minus 2.

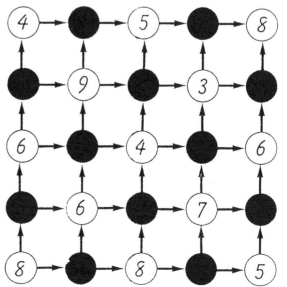

VERBAL What word prefixes all the following?

ATE

MER

LET

MOCK

MY

MATHS The VAT inspector has just given you a refund, and has been weeping every night for a week, since, unfortunately for him, the pounds were transposed for the pence, so you got much more money. Upon receipt of the cheque, you run round to the bank, cash it and spend £2.22. You now look at your cheque and find that the money left over is exactly twice the value of the cheque which you ought to have received. How much did the VAT inspector really owe you?

MISCELLANEOUS A clock is correct at midnight but loses 1½ minutes per hour. You look at the clock and see that it shows 7.30 pm. You recall that you first realized that the clock had stopped exactly half an hour ago. What is the correct time now?

WORKINGS

TRIVIA

1 Which famous character did Basil Rathbone portray in 14 films from 1939 to 1946?

2 What does the abbreviation 'IQ' stand for?

3 Which character's favourite (and indeed only) food is 'cow pie'?

4 What do rhubarb and asparagus have in common, apart from being vegetables?

5 What famous run occurs at St Moritz?

ANSWERS

LOGIC   Sally like fives, sixes, sevens and eights. She does not like ones, twos or threes. Will she like tens?

DIAGRAMMATIC   The letters of *PAPUA* are in the diagram. How many different ways are there of creating the word from these letters, that is, if we assume each *A*, *U* or *P* are unique. Once a group of letters have been used they cannot be re-used in another order. Try numbering the letters.

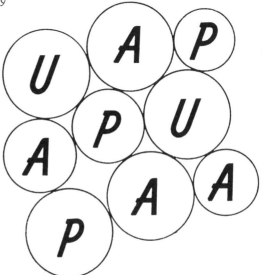

VERBAL The word *FLAME* is written here both horizontally and vertically. Use the following letters to complete the square so that another acceptable word begins with the *L* of *FLAME*, another with the *A* and so on. Here are the letters:

E E E E E I V V N N R R R T T G

```
F L A M E
L
A
M
E
```

MATHS A desperate man raids his child's piggy bank. To his surprise, he finds £83.52 inside. It is made up of 2p, 5p, 10p, 20p and 50p coins. He knows that there is exactly the same number of each kind of coin. How many of each coin are there in the piggy bank?

MISCELLANEOUS If an aeroplane flies out at 120 mph and back at 240 mph what is its average speed?

WORKINGS

TRIVIA

1 What was King Arthur's sword called?

2 In which year did the Great Fire of London start?

3 In which novel does the Earnshaw family appear?

4 In which country did Gruyère cheese originate?

5 What is the nickname of the Arsenal football team?

ANSWERS

LOGIC Can you discover the reasoning and then find the missing numbers?

CAT (HEU) 541

PIG (RLM) 236

DOG (MQL) ???

DIAGRAMMATIC Two planets are in orbit around a sun. They now form a straight line with each other and that luminary. If the orbital speeds of the planets are 33 years and 3 years and if both move in a clockwise direction, when will they next form a straight line with each other and the sun?

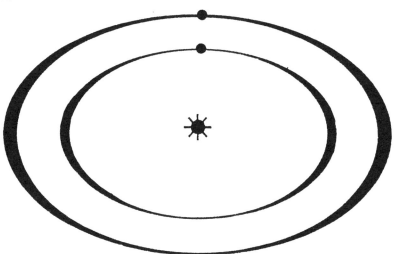

VERBAL What word prefixes all the following?

AL

ED

HEAD

HER

HOM

TEN

MATHS A train travelled from station A to station B. Its outward speed was 105 mph and its return speed was 21 mph over exactly the same distance. What was its average speed for the whole journey?

MISCELLANEOUS In a factory there are four cog wheels. The largest cog wheel has 189 teeth, the next cog has 56 teeth, the next 23 teeth and the smallest cog has 12 teeth. They are now in the start position. How many revolutions will the second-largest cog make before they are back in this position?

WORKINGS

TRIVIA

1 What is the common musical name of a quint, a medieval-sounding interval?

2 Which group of people are bound by the Hippocratic oath?

3 Who invented the revolver?

4 What is afrormosia?

5 Upon what surface is a fresco painted?

ANSWERS

LOGIC If a horse is worth £25, a cat is worth £60 and a dog is worth £21, how much is a goat worth?

DIAGRAMMATIC In the diagram each symbol has been given a value. The numbers are the totals of the values of those symbols in each column or row. What should replace the question mark?

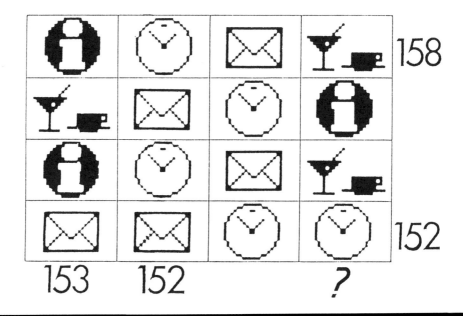

VERBAL You must turn *LAMB* to *PORK* in six steps, changing one letter and making a new word each time.

LAMB

. . . .

. . . .

. . . .

. . . .

. . . .

PORK

MATHS At a chic discotheque, the total takings for the night were £1457. The owner knows that there were more than one and less than 47 people present. How many people were there, and how much did each spend that night?

MISCELLANEOUS A fire engine is travelling 45 miles to a fire at a speed of 74 mph. It has a tank which holds 100 gallons of water. It has developed a leak of 5 gallons per hour. The fire engine will need 95 gallons of water to put out the fire. Will it achieve this?

WORKINGS

TRIVIA

1 Which vitamin is necessary to help blood to clot?

2 Which artery supplies blood to the heart and neck?

3 In which year did Ernest Hemingway win a Nobel Prize?

4 Where would the hammer, anvil and stirrup be found?

5 When a metal is galvanized, with what is it coated?

ANSWERS

LOGIC   A small private bus has four seats upstairs and four seats downstairs. Mrs Black is sitting below Mr Green. Mr Jones is sitting at the rear of the bus. Mr Brown is seated directly behind Mrs Black, while Mr Smith is sitting directly below Mr Jones. Mrs Peters is seated behind Mr Green and in front of Mrs Taylor. Assuming that all seats are occupied and that the last passenger is Mrs White, where is she sitting?

DIAGRAMMATIC   Here is the plan of a flattened cube. Can you tell us which of the cubes below it cannot be made from the plan?

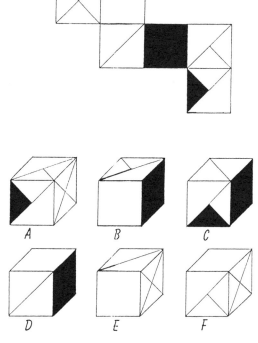

A   B   C

D   E   F

VERBAL   Which word of four letters can be added to these words to form other English words?

Dream Long Ice

MATHS   A car travels a distance of 40 miles at a speed of 40 mph. It covers 40 miles per gallon and has a total tank capacity of 40 gallons. However, it has developed a leak from its tank. It will cover 40 miles, but its tank will be dry at the end. How much petrol does it lose per hour?

MISCELLANEOUS   Here is a message in code. It has been placed in blocks of five letters and punctuation has been missed out. Break the code and read the message:

**BDSJU JDJTB NBOXI PLOPX
TUIFX BZCVU DBOUE SJWFU
IFDBS**

WORKINGS

TRIVIA

1 Where did the Olympic Games take place in 1972?

2 Sitting Bull was a famous chieftain of which Indian tribe?

3 By what process do liquids pass through a porous membrane?

4 What is a catamaran?

5 In what year was the summit of Mount Everest first reached?

ANSWERS

LOGIC If six is worth 11, eight is worth one, seven is worth five and 11 is also worth five, what is 1000 worth?

DIAGRAMMATIC Here is a peculiar dartboard. You have three darts with which to score exactly 88. Each dart must hit the board and score. A dart can enter a segment more than once and each segment is to be regarded as different. How many different ways are there of scoring 88? Once a group of segments has been used it cannot be re-used in another order.

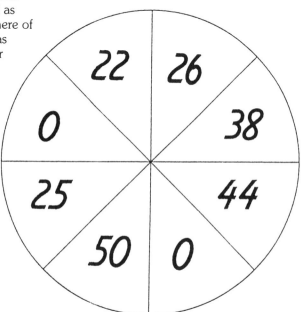

VERBAL There is a set of words here which has been mingled together. Fortunately, the letters are still in the same order as they appear in the words and two words are mingled on each line. You have to 'un-mingle' and tell us the words.

HFRAIGUNHTETENDED
WOEBIGESHETY
SLESNEOPOZEY
EFAGLELIGHT

MATHS Having rented an ill-fated speedboat, you find yourself at the edge of a waterfall, trying to get back. You have seen an island some 21 miles back and can maintain a speed of 16 mph. The current is dragging you back at 9 mph, and as a result you are using 10 gallons of fuel every hour. If your tank contains 31 gallons of fuel when you begin your attempted escape will you survive?

MISCELLANEOUS Assuming that Ben Hur was a real-life figure, do you think he would have been able to break the speed of sound in the great chariot race?

WORKINGS

TRIVIA

1 What is oakum?

2 Which French writer was famous for his short stories, including one about a necklace?

3 In which country would you find the Coptic Church?

4 Which actress had the original name of Harlean Carpenter?

5 What is a divine being or spiritual force called in the Shinto religion?

ANSWERS

22nd Round

LOGIC A supermarket has found that it has been losing shopping trolleys, and has decided to make a real effort to get the trolleys back. As a result, they have created 'The Great Shopping Trolley Race'. You race with your trolley to the car and return with it empty to exactly where you started. You cover the distance to the car at 120 feet per minute. You empty the trolley and return to the shop with the empty trolley at a speed of 960 feet per minute. What was your average speed for the whole journey?

DIAGRAMMATIC In the square are three of the letters of the word *COMET*. You have to fill this with the letters of the word in such a way that no lines, vertical, horizontal or diagonal, of any number of squares contain the same letter.

O				
		C		
	E			

VERBAL

Here is a series of words with a space in the brackets between them. A letter is to be placed between the brackets. The letter should change the words to the left and right of the brackets to other words when it is substituted for the third letter from the beginning in each word. The letters in the brackets, when read downwards, form another word and that is the word we require.

PERT   (   )   LIFT

GOON   (   )   ROMAN

FLAT   (   )   STUNG

DOLE   (   )   CORE

MATHS

A petrol tanker drives along at a steady 30 mph. At the moment it began to move someone put a hole in its tank and ignited the petrol. The flames are following it at a speed of 25 mph. After 26 miles it stops. How long will it be before the flames reach the tanker?

MISCELLANEOUS

Solve this riddle:

My first is in Most but not in Many,
My second is in Pound and also in Penny.
My third is in Sail but not in Ship,
My fourth is in Thrash but never in Whip,
My fifth is in Sink but not in Bath,
My whole up the chimney will make its path.
What am I?

WORKINGS

TRIVIA

1 In which African country would you find Kananga?

2 Of whom, in Greek mythology, was Phaedra the wife?

3 What breed of animal is a duroc?

4 From which plant does the drug atropine come?

5 In which year did Hector Berlioz die?

ANSWERS

23rd | Round

LOGIC Discover the relationship between the numbers in the brackets and those outside them and then tell us what should replace the question marks. The letters are there to help with the explanation.

```
A B C D E F G H I
1 4 9 (4 4 3) 3 0 3
2 2 8 (4 4 2) 2 2 4
7 5 6 (? ? ?) 2 4 2
```

DIAGRAMMATIC A planet revolves around a sun once every 14.5 years. An asteroid has taken up a position which allows its orbit to intersect that of the planet. The asteroid completes an orbit once every 56 years. Both move in the direction indicated in the diagram and the asteroid began its orbit when it was 51.42875 degrees away from the intersection point. When, if ever, will the planet and the asteroid collide?

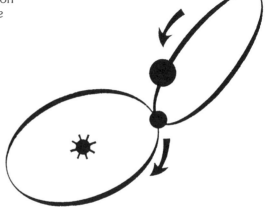

VERBAL   Here is a phrase. Use every letter of the phrase and rearrange them to form the names of three birds.

An eager slight walk

MATHS   Two men named Fred and Bill have a speedboat race over a distance of one mile. Bill loses by 100 metres. Fred says he will race again, this time starting 150 metres behind the starting line. If both the speeds are exactly the same as before, who will win the race this time?

MISCELLANEOUS   If a man without brothers or sisters looks at a photograph and states that the picture is of a man who is his grandson's grandfather's grandson's father, to which relative will he be referring?

WORKINGS

TRIVIA

1 Which German composer, born in 1928, wrote *Gruppen* and *Ylem*?

2 Which Japanese town was the scene of the peace treaty which ended the Sino-Japanese War in 1895?

3 Who was the Greek goddess of fortune?

4 To which other animal is the cacomistle related?

5 Where would you find an astrocyte?

ANSWERS

LOGIC An eccentric diamond merchant decided to give away £50 worth of free diamonds to each male in his town, and to each female £75 worth. There were 500 adults in the town. However, suspecting a catch, only one-half the men claimed their diamonds, and only one-third of the women. By how much was the diamond merchant out of pocket at the end of the exercise?

DIAGRAMMATIC Follow the arrows in the diagram and tell us how many legal ways there are of getting from A to B.

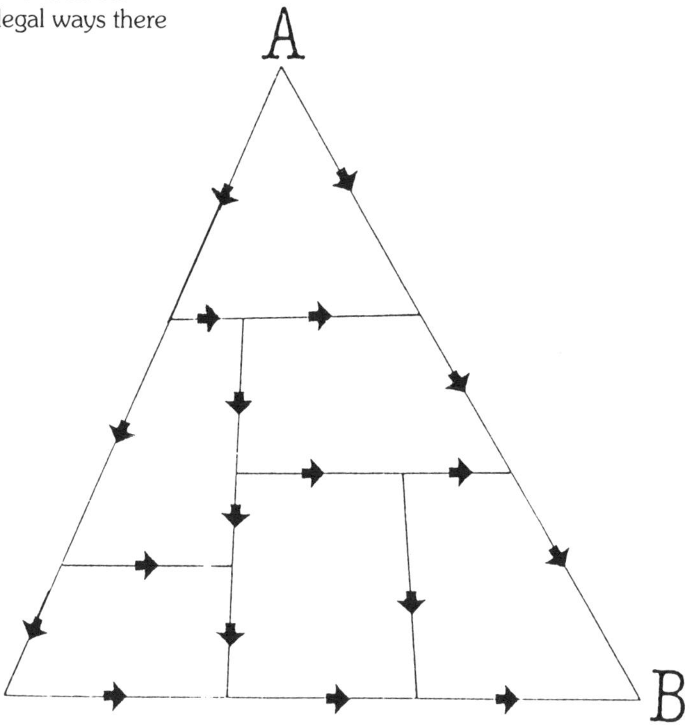

VERBAL   At least three of the same letter have been removed from each of the words below. If you replace the letter in each word you will have your answer. All the other letters are in a mixed-up order. Here are the letters of the words:

TRVRN

RSVRO

PRNNO

RLSWN

MATHS   You go on holiday with your cine camera and 2456 feet of film. We know how you take your movie shots and, bearing the simple rule in mind, realize that every scene is exactly the same footage in length. You take less than 100 scenes but more than four. How many scenes did you take and how much film did you use?

MISCELLANEOUS   Which letter should be used to complete this square of letters?

A B C N

F G G T

J O P ?

WORKINGS

TRIVIA

1 What is celebrated in England each year on 31 October?

2 What, in computer parlance, is PROM?

3 Which Jewish festival is celebrated on Tishri 10?

4 What is borne on an insect's metathorax?

5 Which initials, according to the Bible, were inscribed above Christ on the cross?

ANSWERS

LOGIC You break your watch while on the beach, but since there is a copious quantity of sand available, you decide to make an hourglass. You know that your hourglass was correct at midnight, but it's been losing 15 minutes every hour. It now shows 3 am and stopped exactly one and a half hours ago. Is it 5.30 am and time to get up?

DIAGRAMMATIC Look at the signpost, work out the reasoning and tell us what should replace the question mark.

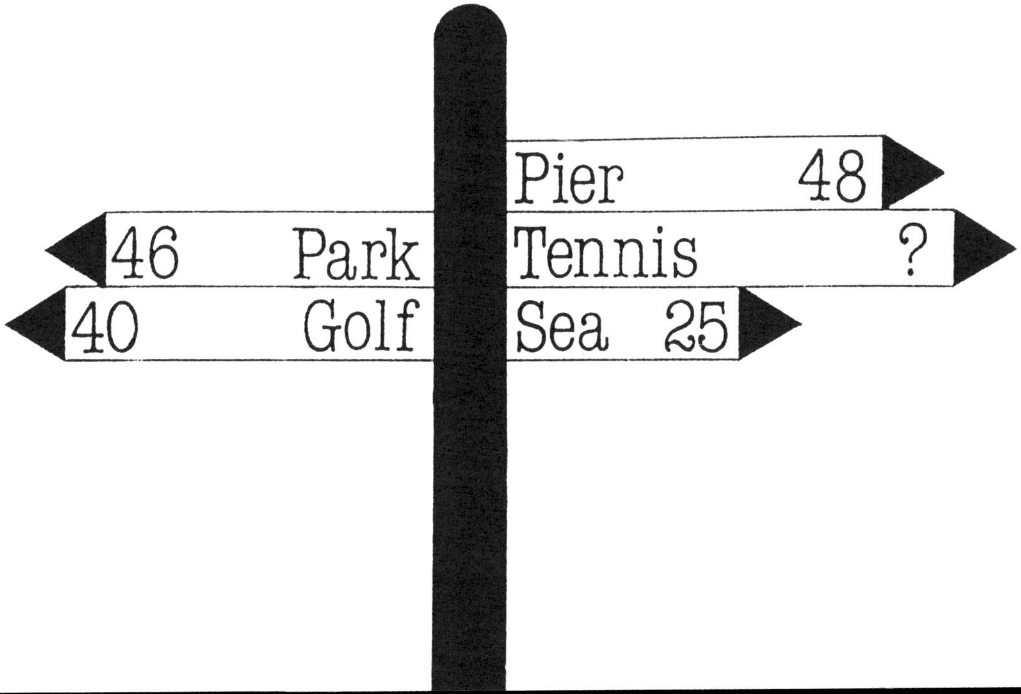

46   Park

40   Golf

Pier   48

Tennis   ?

Sea   25

VERBAL   Here is a series of words with brackets between them. A letter is placed in the brackets. The letter should change the words to the left and right of the brackets to other words when it is substituted for the second letter from the beginning of the word. The letters in the brackets, when read downwards, now form another, somewhat agreeable, word.

ASTER	( )	FRAME
BOND	( )	STEN
FARE	( )	WEND
ALP	( )	TEAR
ASK	( )	GIN
BLEED	( )	FLY
TIE	( )	ROAD

MATHS   Your Christmas savings come to £20.91, made up of an equal number of 2p, 5p and 10p coins. How many of each coin do you have?

MISCELLANEOUS   Halley's comet has assumed a rather peculiar orbit. It has begun to circle the sun, and takes 22 years to make one full revolution. It is exactly 180 degrees away from the intersection point with earth's orbit. The earth has slowed down, and now takes 55 years to complete an orbit, moving in a clockwise direction. When will the two heavenly bodies next meet?

WORKINGS

TRIVIA

1 Which range of American mountains contains Mount Rainier as its highest peak?

2 In which year did Louis Blériot make the first flight across the Channel?

3 What is a kris?

4 Which Turkish sultan captured Constantinople in AD 1453?

5 What is the modern name of the town known to the ancient Greeks as Syene?

ANSWERS

LOGIC   Here we have the name of an imaginary author written in code. The title of the most famous work of this author is *A Treatise on Cannibalism*. You must break the code and read the message.

54 55 58 41

42 55 54 45

DIAGRAMMATIC   What should replace the question mark in the diagram so that the bottom set of scales balance, assuming that the other two sets are in perfect equilibrium?

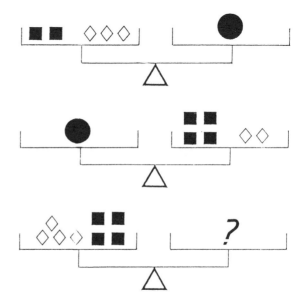

VERBAL   Here is another word written out both horizontally and vertically. Complete the wordsquare in such a way that it reads both downwards and across with good English words. This time you must only use the letters of the word given to complete the square plus *one* additional letter.

R A V E
A
V
E

MATHS   What number when divided by 12 will use every number from 1 to 9 once and once only?

MISCELLANEOUS   You are given the following letters: five As, three Ls, three Ms, two Ps, two Es and one R. You must use these letters to form a wordsquare like that given earlier in the verbal section of this round.

WORKINGS

TRIVIA

1 What was a yamen?

2 Where in Central Africa is the Copper Belt?

3 What is the present name of Lake Nyasa?

4 What is the full name of Colonel Gaddafi?

5 What was the original name of Gracie Fields?

ANSWERS

27th | Round

LOGIC   Your best friend has bought you a present for your birthday, namely a bottle of wine. He knows that you are particularly fond of old claret and, having come into a fortune, has purchased a bottle of 1842 Chateau Latour, 1er Grand Cru Classé. Do you think he was cheated if he paid over £30 for the bottle?

DIAGRAMMATIC   The diagram shows an arrangement of numbers. You must always start at the centre two and then collect a further three numbers. These are added together. You can move upwards, downwards or across but never diagonally from square to touching square. How many different ways are there of attaining the total 57? A route which can be reversed is classed as a second route.

```
                          26
                     18  18  11
                 26  26  11  18  18
             11  18  26   2  11  18  26
                 26  18  11  18  18
                     11  26  26
                          11
```

BAGS MAKER WORT

MATHS Can you replace the brackets and the mathematical symbols to the left of the equals sign so that the equation works out?

5 3 2 23 = 40

MISCELLANEOUS Which letter continues this series of letters?

Q S C   W D V   E F B   R G ?

WORKINGS

TRIVIA

1 What is the name of the strait between Puerto Rica and the Dominican Republic linking the Atlantic with the Caribbean?

2 What is a razoo?

3 Which pope had the original name of Giuliano della Rovere?

4 What was the name of the 4th-century BC Athenian courtesan who was mistress of Alexander the Great?

5 What kind of astral body is Eros?

ANSWERS

28th | Round

LOGIC Two teenagers on the beach have a personal stereo unit between them. They work out that they will allow each other to listen for exactly 48 minutes and they will take it in turn. Suddenly, some more friends arrive—four more, to be precise. They all want an equal time for listening to the stereo in the same amount of time as the first two had already agreed. How long will each be able to listen?

DIAGRAMMATIC In the diagram are the letters of the word *VENEZUELA*. You must start at the bottom *V*, move upwards and from left to right, and collect the nine letters of the word. How many different ways can be found to achieve this?

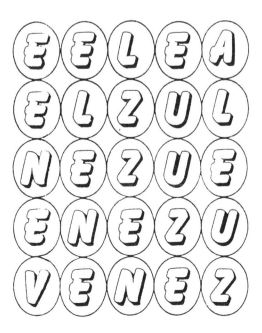

VERBAL   Replace the first letter of each word on either side of the brackets with another letter. This will form two different English words. Then place this letter in the brackets. When you read all the letters in the brackets downwards you will find that they form a birdlike word.

COMB	( )	BENT
APT	( )	TAR
OTTER	( )	SPEND
MOAT	( )	MATCH
FIR	( )	RUNT
LAME	( )	FIGHT

MATHS   Of two taps on a bath, the cold fills the bath in 13 minutes with the plug in and the hot tap off, while the hot tap takes 7 minutes under similar circumstances. It takes 12 minutes to empty the bath when the plug is removed. With both taps on and the plug out when will the bath be full?

MISCELLANEOUS   A delivery of food arrived at your holiday hotel. One-sixteenth of the food was canned dog food, one-eighth was canned cat food, three-tenths contained rat poison and 60 tins were damaged. There were 63 cans of tinned rhubarb and these were undamaged. Can you tell us how many cans were in the consignment?

WORKINGS

TRIVIA

1 What was the surname of the first president of Czechoslovakia?

2 What was Peter's Pence, which was abolished by Henry VIII in 1534?

3 Which Pope instituted the Fourth Crusade in 1202?

4 What is oriental topaz?

5 Which Welsh county has its administrative headquarters at Mold?

ANSWERS

LOGIC What letter is the next in this series?

E Z D V F ?

DIAGRAMMATIC Can you arrange the following numbers in the grid in such a way that each segment of three numbers totals 36 while each circle of numbers totals 96? Here are the numbers:

9 9 10 10 11 11 11 11 11 11 12 12 12 12 12 12 13 13 13 13 14 14 16 16

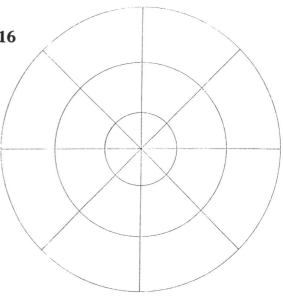

VERBAL   What word, when placed after 'gavel' and before 'red' will form two good, new words?

MATHS   Your house is 30 miles away from the fire station and is on fire. The fire engine is travelling at 20 mph. This one has a leaking water tank and is losing 10 gallons every hour. The tank contains, when full, 20 gallons of water. Will they put out your fire if they need exactly 8 gallons of water?

MISCELLANEOUS   At least three of the same letters have been removed from each of the words below. If you replace the letter in each word you will have your answer. All of the other letters are in a mixed-up order. Here are the letters of the words:

ASIE

ERAE

BASNIE

NAMEE

ENEAS

WORKINGS

TRIVIA

1 What is a rondeau?

2 What relationship to Mohammed was the caliph, Husain, who died in AD 680?

3 In which Canadian province would you find Cape Breton Island?

4 From which flower does pyrethrum come?

5 Which river is named the Duna in Hungarian?

ANSWERS

LOGIC On a Sunday morning you are driving along in your car at a leisurely 21 mph and using petrol at a rate of 21 miles per gallon. You have 21 gallons in the tank. However, your tank is leaking petrol at a rate of 4.25 gallons every hour. How far can you travel before you run out of petrol?

DIAGRAMMATIC Two planets are in orbit around a sun in a strange solar system. Here each year is five months long. Both move in the same direction and are now in line with each other and the sun. One takes 6 years to complete an orbit while the other takes 25 years. When in their months will they next form a straight line with each other and the sun?

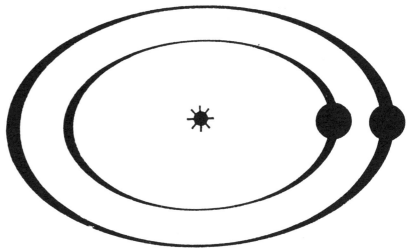

VERBAL Here is a series of words with a space in the brackets between them. A letter is to be placed inside this to change the words to the left and right of the brackets to other words when it is substituted for the first letter of each word. The letters in the brackets, when read downwards, will form a new word.

MAST	( )	MATCH
AMBER	( )	**ADDER**
SOUGHT	( )	**HAIL**
PAIN	( )	**LOT**
PLATE	( )	**CAVES**

MATHS In your piggy bank you have a total of £392.70, made up of 165 of each of six different kinds of English coin. All the coins are in circulation today. Can you tell us which coins they are?

MISCELLANEOUS It takes the hot tap 10 minutes to fill your bath while it takes the other 16 minutes. However, you have unwittingly left the plug out and the bath will empty in 40 minutes with the taps off. If both taps are on full, how long, if ever, will it take the bath to fill?

WORKINGS

TRIVIA

1 What name is given to a dagger in printing?

2 Of which Austrian province is Graz the capital?

3 Which Bohemian successfully led the Hussite rebellion against Emperor Sigismund?

4 In botany, what name is given to the thin outer layer of a mushroom cap?

5 What, in imperial Russia, was the Duma?

ANSWERS

LOGIC Four men are being questioned concerning the robbery of a mansion. Their statements are as follows:

Bruiser: 'Birdy did it.'
John: 'Bruiser did it.'
Birdy: 'Bruiser lied when he said I did it.'
Smithy: 'I didn't do it.'

The police know that only one statement is true. Who committed the heinous crime?

DIAGRAMMATIC In the diagram you have to start from one of the corners and collect five numbers by following the lines. The five numbers will include your corner number and you cannot use another corner. No retracing of steps is allowed. By adding the five numbers together there are several different ways of making a total of 26. How many are there?

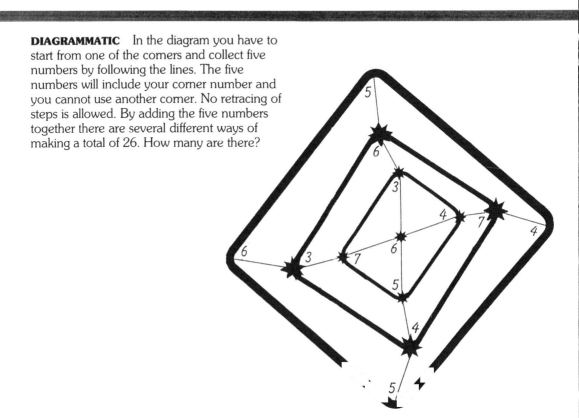

VERBAL   Can you find a three-letter suffix to go after each of these sets of letters?

GAT RAT LAT WIT

MATHS   A cricketer's average in his first 18 innings was 16.5 runs. After a further eight innings his average had increased to 32.5 runs. What was his average for the last eight innings only?

MISCELLANEOUS   While visiting the zoo you come across an extremely strange inventory of animals. Not only do the numbers quoted against the various attractions bear no relevance to the actual numbers of the animals, but one of the numbers has been completely omitted! You sit down with your packed lunch and attempt to work out the logic behind it. Just forget the vowels.

ZEBRA: 9
LION: 6
TIGRESS: 15
ANTELOPE: ?

What is the distance which should go with *ANTELOPE*?

WORKINGS

TRIVIA

1 Which bay was the site of the Battle of the Nile in 1798?

2 From what stone is the Taj Mahal constructed?

3 What is the name of the artistic style associated with the reign of the Japanese emperor, Yoshihito (1912–26)?

4 What, in Hebrew, is the meaning of 'Hallelujah'?

5 What is the common name for the drug, lysergic acid diethylamide?

ANSWERS

LOGIC   If a CAT costs £7 and a PIG costs £1, while a DOG costs £5.50, how much will an ELK cost?

DIAGRAMMATIC   Here are some numbers which, when placed in the empty squares of the grid, will ensure that each vertical, horizontal and main diagonal line total 130. Can you find where each number goes?

21 21 22 22 26 30 30 31 31

32	29	32	5	32
34				4
33				19
11				55
20	20	20	50	20

Which two words of the same four letters will replace the blanks in this sentence?

A frog BLANK in terror out of the restaurant which was above the baker's BLANK.

What should replace the question marks inside the brackets?

359 (983)
104 (114)
222 (???)

Can you solve and read this cryptic message?

EVA LST AFA EBO TNA HTE ERF RET TEB

WORKINGS

TRIVIA

1 Which borough of north-west Greater London has a population of 256,500?

2 What is the name of the third largest Hawaiian island?

3 Which French novelist wrote *A la Recherche du Temps Perdu*?

4 Which German idealist philosopher wrote *Critique of Pure Reason*?

5 What is pulque?

ANSWERS

33rd | Round

LOGIC You driving along the motorway with your side-lights and head-lights on. Your visibility is fair. Suddenly, all your electrics fail and you are stranded in the fast lane. However, the other traffic manages to avoid you without any difficulty, and you eventually get home safely. Why was it so easy to avoid you?

DIAGRAMMATIC In the diagram each symbol has a value. The total of the values in each column and line are represented by the figures alongside them. Can you tell us what should replace the question mark?

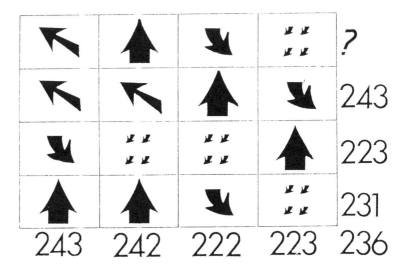

What word of your letters can be added to the front of each of these words to create other English words?

BEAM STONE BILL BOOK

MATHS Can you replace the mathematical symbols in this equation? Forget the brackets this time.

5 6 7 3 8 = 5

MISCELLANEOUS Place one letter in the brackets so that it finishes the left-hand word and begins the right-hand one. Then you can read another word downwards.

PAR ( ) CORN

SIT ( ) HIP

DEN ( ) HIS

CAR ( ) CAD

BEE ( ) AIL

WORKINGS

TRIVIA

1 What is a phasmid?

2 Which element has the atomic number 81?

3 What is the name of the second largest city in Algeria?

4 What was the name of the Inca ruler who was murdered by his half-brother Atahualpa?

5 Which English actress played opposite Sir Henry Irving and corresponded with George Bernard Shaw?

ANSWERS

34th | Round

LOGIC   A man sets out to fly from one city to another. On the first day he covers one-half of the total distance, on the second day he covers one-quarter of what is left, on the third day he covers one-sixth of the remainder and on the fourth day, after covering half the final distance to the city, finds that he is 246¼ miles away. How far has he travelled to this point?

DIAGRAMMATIC   Follow the arrows from the bottom left-hand corner to the top right-hand corner of the diagram, adding numbers as you go. The black circles are all worth minus five. Bearing this in mind, how many ways are there of scoring 7?

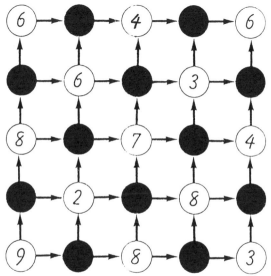

VERBAL Can you change *KICK* to *MULE* in five steps? You change one letter at each step and ensure that the change makes another English word.

KICK

. . . .

. . . .

. . . .

MULE

MATHS What is the next number in this mathematical series?

2 4 6 10 14 22 26 ?

MISCELLANEOUS In a field there are seven pigs, 38 cows, 45 bulls and 55 donkeys. How many horses are there?

WORKINGS

TRIVIA

1 What name is given to the hot southerly wind blowing from about March to May, especially in Egypt?

2 What, according to historical sources, happened in the Teuterburgerwald in AD 9?

3 In which year was the United Nations Organization founded?

4 What is a buttonball?

5 Which German poet wrote 'Des Knaben Wunderhorn' (1805–8)?

ANSWERS

LOGIC   Your unreliable watch has begun to lose 15 minutes every hour and is now showing 6 am. You recall that it stopped 2 hours ago. If it was correct at midnight, at what time did it stop?

DIAGRAMMATIC   In the diagram you start at the centre S and move from square to touching square collecting four letters. You move upwards, downwards or across but never diagonally. By following the rules, how many ways are there of collecting the letters of the word *SKIN* by following different routes?

```
              N
          K   I   N
      I   K   N   N   N
  I   K   I   S   I   K   I
      N   N   K   I   N
          K   I   N
              K
```

VERBAL   Here is a series of words with a space in the brackets between them. A letter is to be placed inside the brackets. This letter should change the words to the left and right of the brackets to other words when it is substituted for the second letter of each word. The letters in the brackets, when read downwards, will form a new word.

CLAW   ( )   BLAND
COME   ( )   CUT
ORE   ( )   ACT
SHRUB ( )   AMID
CLUB   ( )   STALL

MATHS   A cricketer's average in his first 12 innings was 14 runs. After a further 16 innings his average had increased to 18 runs. What was his average for the last 16 innings only?

MISCELLANEOUS   What is the next in this series of letters?

ER EN AR AR UP ?

WORKINGS

TRIVIA

1 What was a pythia?

2 To which human organ does the thalamus relate?

3 Which queen of Egypt came before Thutmose III?

4 Who was the Roman goddess of the hearth?

5 Where would you find Butung?

ANSWERS

36th | Round

LOGIC   A tramp discovers that he can make one full cigarette from 16 stubs. If he finds 280 stubs on the floor after a hard day's work, how many full cigarettes can he make in total?

DIAGRAMMATIC   In the diagram all the vertical and horizontal lines plus the two main diagonals will total 240 when the missing numbers are inserted. If we give you the numbers, can you do it? Here are the numbers:

41 42 43 44 48 52 53 54 55

54	74	53	3	56
76				4
55				41
15				97
40	17	43	98	42

VERBAL   Which five-letter word can be added to the end of the first word and to the beginning of the second word to create two other good English words?

LOAD (   ) FLY

MATHS   A train travelled from station A to B at a speed of 210 mph. Its return journey from B to A, however, was completed at a speed of 40 mph, due to an engine breakdown. What was the train's average speed?

MISCELLANEOUS   Your watch is correct at midnight but gains 19 minutes per hour. You look at the clock and see that it shows 10.32 am. You recall that you first realized the clock had stopped exactly a quarter of an hour ago. What is the correct time now?

WORKINGS

TRIVIA

1 What was a ceorl?

2 Which lake in Italy was the scene of Hannibal's victory over the Romans?

3 Where is Victoria Peak in the Far East?

4 In which film did Peter Cushing play an old doctor just released from the Bastille?

5 Who was the national leader of Argentina at the time of the Falklands War?

ANSWERS

LOGIC Can you break the following code and read the quotation? All the vowels have been replaced with asterisks.

X I * O * O E * * C U X * O U I * U
S * D L

DIAGRAMMATIC The top two sets of scales in the diagram are in perfect balance. To make the third set of scales balance, a certain number of black diamonds must be added. How many are there?

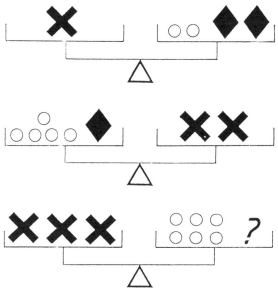

VERBAL   Can you find a three-letter suffix which will go after each of these sets of letters to form words?

GO PROB EMB

MATHS   A jeweller earned £5600 in a week by selling uncut diamonds and rubies. Diamonds cost five times more than rubies. Of the 1500 gems sold, only a fraction were diamonds. Diamonds were sold at a price of £200 for 25. What fraction of the total gems were diamonds?

MISCELLANEOUS   A ship is battling against a current to safety. It is 40 miles from an island. It is travelling at 22 mph but the rate of flow of the stream is 4 mph against the ship. The ship uses 26 gallons of fuel every hour and has a tank capacity of 58 gallons. Will it reach safety?

WORKINGS

TRIVIA

1 What nickname was given to Lord Townshend in the 18th century?

2 On the eastern part of which island is the town of Elounda?

3 Who composed *Ma Vlast*?

4 Who wrote *Les Mains Sales* in 1948?

5 Where, in geography, would you find a cirque?

ANSWERS

38th | Round

LOGIC   There are four cog wheels. The largest cog has 208 teeth, the next cog 110 teeth, the next 55 teeth and the smallest cog has 26 teeth. The cogs start to turn. How many revolutions will the smallest cog make before they are all back to the start position?

DIAGRAMMATIC   Arrange the following numbers in the diagram in such a way that each segment of three numbers totals 207. Here are the numbers:

66 66 67 68 67 68
68 68 69 69 69 69
68 73 73 71 70 71
68 70 70 69 70 69

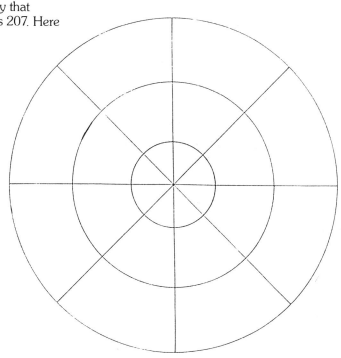

VERBAL   Can you find the two five words of the same five letters which can be used to replace the blanks in this sentence?

After melting down his BLANK to make tools the peasant crosses his land and BLANK his meagre crop.

MATHS   A man cashed a cheque at a bank and discovered that the bank cashier had transposed the pounds for pence and the pence for pounds on the cheque, thus giving him far more money. He bought goods for £7.45 and discovered that he now had exactly twice the amount of money that the original cheque was for. For how much was the original cheque?

MISCELLANEOUS   Your clock has just struck 10 and, having timed it with your stopwatch, you discover that, from the first to the last stroke, it takes exactly 9 seconds. How long will it take to strike 12?

WORKINGS

TRIVIA

1 For what would a diva be famous?

2 Who invented the seed-drill in the 18th century?

3 On which island would you find the 'Baths of Aphrodite'?

4 What kind of bird is a sawbill?

5 For what practice were the Naga people notorious?

ANSWERS

LOGIC   You have a vivarium filled with insects. There are insects with 12 wings and some with 14; insects with 16 wings and some with only four. You know that you have an equal number of insects of each type and you know that you have a total of 8694 wings. How many insects of each type do you have?

DIAGRAMMATIC   Look at the diagram, discover the values of the symbols by comparing them with the numbers next to each column and row and then tell us what should replace the question mark.

☆	✶	✶	✩ ✩	
✶	✶	✩ ✩	☆	
☆	☆	✶	✶	162
✶	✶	✶	✩ ✩	148
158	167	?	135	155

VERBAL Two letters placed in the brackets will change the letters either side of the brackets to words. When read downwards the letters in the brackets will form another word. What is this word?

SE   ( )   **ME**

AM   ( )   **AT**

BAL ( )   **TIRE**

MATHS In a 100-metre race Peter beats John by 10 metres. The race is now run again, with Peter starting 11 metres behind the starting line. Who wins the race this time?

MISCELLANEOUS A farmer earned a certain sum last week by selling birds. Ducklings cost twice as much as chicks but, of 100 birds sold, only one-quarter were ducklings. Ducklings were sold at a price of £4 for 10. How much money did he earn that week?

WORKINGS

TRIVIA

1 Who was the subject of the Pragmatic Sanction which was signed by many before the War of Austrian Succession in the 18th century?

2 What is a cistron?

3 Who played Ramses II in the film *The Ten Commandments*?

4 Which 19th-century composer wrote the overture *Rienzi*?

5 Which is the main largest island of the Philippines?

ANSWERS

LOGIC Five cricketers score as follows: Andy scores 16 more runs than Bill and Bill scores 13 less runs than Charles. We also know that Eric scores 492 more runs than Dave, Charles scores 920 more runs than Eric and that the total runs scored by Bill and Eric is 500. What is the total scored by the five cricketers during the match?

DIAGRAMMATIC Look at the diagram and select a corner number. You may only use one corner. Then moving along the lines add the corner value to four other values. You cannot backtrack. Once you have a total of the five numbers you must divide it by the corner number. Now tell us how many times you can score exactly 8.

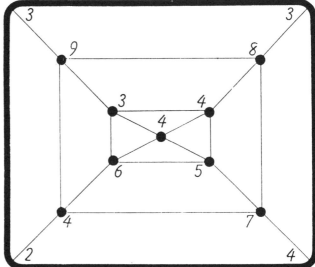

Fill in the missing letters of this wordsquare in such a way that four new words are created which read the same downwards and across. You must use six Es, two Ts, one S, one B and two As plus other letters.

F O R G E
O
R
G
E

What are the four words?

MATHS Can you replace the missing mathematical symbols in this equation? Forget the brackets.

6 2 2 3 5 = 10

MISCELLANEOUS Can you work out the reasoning of this cryptic quotation and tell us what it is?

YRXL YLTSC DN TVRP S YTLRM

WORKINGS

TRIVIA

1 What is soubise?

2 What is a 'Jimmy Woodser'?

3 During which period did dinosaurs flourish?

4 What is a Quashi?

5 Who was the world chess champion from 1969 to 1972?

ANSWERS

LOGIC   A man bought a car for £100. He found he did not like it so he sold it to a friend for £90. The friend managed to sell it for £95 to another friend. The second friend was also a friend of the first man and sold him the car for £80. If the car could always realize £60, what is the most the first man could lose on the deal?

DIAGRAMMATIC   In the diagram the top two sets of scales are in perfect balance. Can you tell us how many hearts are required to replace the question mark on the bottom set?

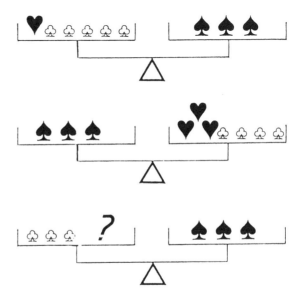

VERBAL   Replace the first letter of each word on either side of the brackets with another letter. This will form two other English words. You must then place the letter in the brackets. When you read all the letters in the brackets downwards you will find that they form a word.

TOME   ( )   FLAP

PATH   ( )   ALIVE

BILL   ( )   FIDDLE

SLOPE   ( )   BARN

DRUNK   ( )   COAST

MATHS   At an old cinema the total takings for the night's entrance fees were £88.90. The manager knows that there was more than 40 but less than 75 people present. Each paid exactly the same entrance fee and no halfpence were accepted. Exactly how many people were there, and what did they each pay?

MISCELLANEOUS   Which word of three letters can be placed between these two words so that it ends the first word and begins the second? In both cases other English words are formed.

POT (   ) LESS

WORKINGS

TRIVIA

1 What was the name of Henry IV before he became king?

2 Where is the Richelieu river?

3 What name (that of a bird) is applied to a person who portends or brings bad luck?

4 Who was the 27th President of the United States of America?

5 What is the name of the largest oasis in the Sahara?

ANSWERS

42nd Round

LOGIC Four cogs are in constant mesh. The largest has 97 teeth, the next 63, the next 54 and the last 14. The cogs start to turn. How many revolutions will the largest cog have to make before they all return to their start position?

DIAGRAMMATIC Using the numbers given, complete the square in the diagram so that each column and row add up to 40, as also do the main diagonals. Here are the numbers to use:

13 8 6 12 13 3 10 4 3

11	0	14	4	11
0				2
10				6
14				16
5	13	2	15	5

VERBAL Complete the following wordsquare so that the words read the same across as downwards.

F I G H T
I
G
H
T

MATHS Can you replace the missing mathematical symbols in this equation? Forget the brackets.

1 10 3 3 40 = 4

MISCELLANEOUS Can you crack this code and read the quotation?

UHF FJRTT DATUBLUY XHFN
XAS CPMFS JS URVTI

WORKINGS

TRIVIA

1 In which country would you find Sergipe?

2 Which Portuguese king secured independence for Portugal?

3 Which French writer wrote *Zazie dans le Metro* in 1959?

4 In which country is the city of Taegu?

5 In which battle in 1644 did the Parliamentarians defeat the Royalists?

ANSWERS

LOGIC A jeweller earned a certain sum last week by selling semi-precious gems. Large gems cost four times as much as small ones but, of the 80 gems sold, only one half were large. Large gems were sold at a price of £64 for 10. How much money did he earn?

DIAGRAMMATIC There are the letters of the word *HAITI* in the grid. Regard each letter as being different and then tell us how many different ways there are of forming the word *HAITI*. Remember that *IAIHT* does not spell *HAITI*!

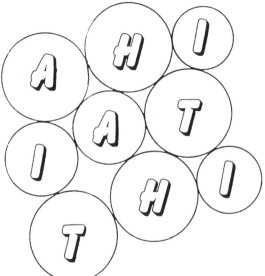

VERBAL   Can you replace the last letter of each of the following words to create another good English word in each case? If you then take all the letters you used you will find that they form a new word themselves. The words in their correct order are:

SHEET PEACE MANE FLAN EIGHTY CORE

What does the word *FLAN* change to?

MATHS   A man sets out to walk from one town to another. On the first day he covers one-quarter of the total distance. On the second day he covers one-third of what was left. On the third he covers one-half of the remaining distance, and on the fourth day he covers one-sixth of the rest. He now has $2\frac{1}{2}$ miles left to go. How far has he travelled up to now?

MISCELLANEOUS   A planet is orbiting the sun in a clockwise direction and will take 26 years to complete the orbit. An asteroid travelling in an anti-clockwise direction is at 120 degrees away from the intersection point and will take 12 years to complete an orbit. How long will it take for the planet and the asteroid to collide?

WORKINGS

TRIVIA

1 Who founded the *Daily Mail* in 1896?

2 Which saint was famous for the production of the Vulgate and whose feast day is 30 September?

3 For what is Albert Bruce Sabin famous?

4 What is the name of the dark, sweet dessert wine made in Sicily, where there is a port of the same name?

5 Which French department has its capital at Valence?

ANSWERS

LOGIC   Here is a series of letters:

O T G C ?

What letter should replace the question mark
and continue the series?

DIAGRAMMATIC   By moving from the bottom
left-hand corner of the diagram to the top right-
hand corner you can collect nine numbers
which will obviously include the first 6 and the
last 9. By using this method, what is the highest
score that can be attained?

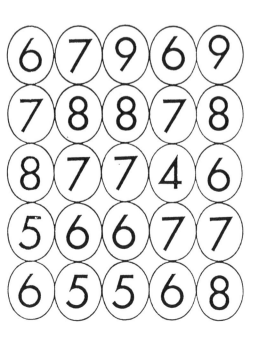

VERBAL   Replace the first letter of each word on either side of the brackets with another letter. This will form two good English words. You must then place the letter in the brackets. When you read all the letters in the brackets downwards you will find that they form a word. What is this word?

ITEM   ( )   WINK
HAT   ( )   CAR
CARROT ( )   LARK
MENT   ( )   BELL
AFFECT   ( )   MAST
FEET   ( )   PEDAL
SLOT   '( )   FLAME
SLATE   ( )   PLASTIC
PEST   ( )   TENT

MATHS   If you have a 15 by 15 square, how many rectangles of any size can you possibly construct?

MISCELLANEOUS   An aircraft leaves Rome for Paris at 2.00 pm and one leaves Rome for London at the same time. Imagine that the distance between Rome and London is 432 miles. If the first plane flies at 110 mph and the second at 140 mph how far apart will they be half an hour before they pass each other?

WORKINGS

TRIVIA

1 Which English dramatist (1882–1937) wrote *Abraham Lincoln* and *Mary Stewart*?

2 What other name was given to modern Greek vernacular, especially Demotic?

3 By what name is the largest of the dark plains on the moon known?

4 What name is given to ceramic compounds with the formula MFe_2O_4?

5 Which Russian nobility ranked immediately below the princes until abolished by Peter the Great?

ANSWERS

LOGIC   The total winnings of a pools syndicate were £6204. There were more than 70 people involved but less than 100. Each person won the same amount in full pounds only. Can you tell us how many people were involved and how much each won?

DIAGRAMMATIC   Here is a strange dartboard. You have five darts with each round and each dart will hit the board and score. A dart can enter a segment more than once, and if the same number appears in another segment this is regarded as being a different number. Following these rules, and remembering that once a group of numbers has been used it cannot be used again in another order, tell us how many different ways there are of scoring 200.

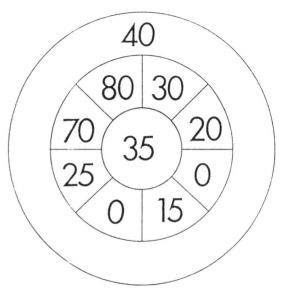

VERBAL A word of five letters can be placed after all of the following to give good, English words in each case. What letter begins this word? Here are the preceding letters:

DE, CON, PRO, EX

MATHS A high-speed train is travelling at 100 mph towards a tunnel. The train is one-tenth of a mile long. The tunnel it is about to enter is exactly 5 miles long. You must predict how long it will take the whole of the train to pass through, from the moment the front of the train enters the tunnel to when the last of the rear emerges.

MISCELLANEOUS The distances on the list below are related to the letters in the words. Find the logic behind the numbers and tell us how far it is to the parks.

COVES: 32,219 metres
BEACH: 218 metres
HOTEL: 82,012 metres
PARKS: ?

WORKINGS

TRIVIA

1 Which northern Spanish village saw the death of Roland in AD 778?

2 Who might wear bowgangs?

3 Which French sculptor and painter is famous for 'Nude Descending a Staircase' (1912)?

4 Where might a kondo perform a robbery?

5 Who was the first aviatrix to cross the Atlantic?

ANSWERS

LOGIC   Here are some numbers:

5 8 7 6 2 9 3

You must insert THREE plus signs so that the total of the sum comes to 220. Where are the plus signs?

DIAGRAMMATIC   If you start at the 26 in the diagram and move either upwards, downwards or across from square to touching square and collect four numbers, how many different ways are there of making a total of 59? You cannot move diagonally but can count a reversed route as being different.

				15		
			5	13	15	
		15	13	5	5	5
	5	15	13	26	15	13	15
		5	5	13	15	5
			13	15	5	
			13			

VERBAL Place THREE letters inside the brackets. The letters must complete a word when added to the end of those to the left of the brackets and complete a second word when added to the front of those to the right of the brackets. When each group of three letters is read downwards another nine-letter word is formed. What is the word?

DE   (   )   **DON**

PA   (   )   **COLITE**

CLOT   (   )   **SIAN**

MATHS In a 220-metre race Jean beats Mary by 20 metres. The race is now run again with Jean starting 22 metres behind the starting line. Who wins the race?

MISCELLANEOUS In a game of eleven players, which lasts for exactly 1 hour 41 minutes, there are 33 reserves who alternate equally with each player in the team. Therefore all the players, including reserves, are on the field for the same amount of time. How long would this time be?

WORKINGS

TRIVIA

1 Who wrote *Juno and the Paycock*?

2 Which scientist wrote *The Sceptical Chymist* in 1661?

3 What is the present name of the Brazilian territory, Guapore?

4 Which legendary beast of enormous size was believed to live off the coast of Norway?

5 From what did the Russian kopek get its name?

ANSWERS

LOGIC   The following group of letters follows a logical sequence. You must work out the logic behind them, and replace the question mark with the relevant letter.

Z, X, C, V, B, N, ?

DIAGRAMMATIC   In a very strange solar system there are only two weeks in a year. The two planets are in orbit around a sun, the first taking 7 years to complete an orbit and the second taking 14 years. They are now in line with each other and their sun and both move in an anti-clockwise direction. When, in this system's weeks, will they next form a straight line with each other and the sun?

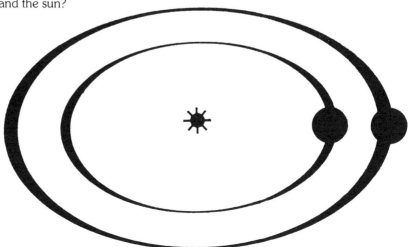

VERBAL Can you extract the names of three composers from this sentence by using every letter?

When do I pack, O Beryl?

MATHS It takes one tap 10 minutes to fill a bath while it takes the other 16 minutes. The plug has been left out, and the bath will empty in 40 minutes with both taps off. If both taps were left full on, however, when, if ever, will the bath be filled?

MISCELLANEOUS A bottle of scent costs £60. The bottle is most ornate and has a value. The scent costs £25 more than the bottle. Can you tell us how much the bottle is worth?

WORKINGS

TRIVIA

1 What is a Santa Gertrudis?

2 What was the real name of the Irish short-story writer and critic, Michael O'Donovan?

3 What was the original meaning of kowtow?

4 Where was the mythical birthplace of Sir Tristram?

5 What is phyllite?

ANSWERS

48th | Round

LOGIC The following letter series contains a
hidden logic. You must work out this logic and
complete the sequence.

A A A U E ?

DIAGRAMMATIC Start at the bottom left-hand
corner of the diagram and follow the arrows to
the top right-hand corner. You collect numbers
as you go, but each black circle is worth minus
one half. What is the highest score you can
attain?

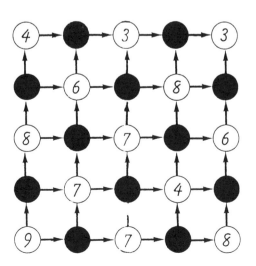

VERBAL   What four-letter word will go between these to form two good English words? The first will end with this word and the second will start with it.

RING (   ) ROPE

MATHS   A car travels a distance of 70 miles at a speed of 35 mph. It burns petrol at a rate of 20 miles per gallon and has a total tank capacity of 15 gallons. It has developed a leak. The car covers 70 miles, but its tank is dry at the end. How much petrol was it using per hour?

MISCELLANEOUS   A gifted child was asked how many pens he had in his case. He replied that he had four-fifths of their number plus four-fifths of a pen. He added that no pen was broken. How many pens did he actually have?

WORKINGS

TRIVIA

1 What was the name of the communications satellite launched in 1965, providing telephone linkage between the United States and Europe?

2 In which sport would you hear the term 'sixte'?

3 What is the meaning of 'eupepsia'?

4 Which singer accompanied James Mason in the film *Journey to the Centre of the Earth*?

5 Which English king was called the 'Sailor King'?

ANSWERS

49th | Round

LOGIC Can you break the code and find the quotation which is in the original language?

OER EPX EFI TRA SIL AUQ

DIAGRAMMATIC How many different ways are there of scoring 112 by using four darts at a time? Each dart must score but can land in a segment more than once. When a group of numbers have been used they cannot be used again in any other order.

VERBAL Can you extract the names of three creatures from this sentence by using every letter?

I, poor Dante, lost more to it.

MATHS What is the next number in this series?

(1,8,9) (4,7,9) (9,4,7) (16,6,?)

MISCELLANEOUS A train is travelling to Bulgaria at a constant speed of 90 mph. On the way back, over the same distance and packed with cargo, the train could only manage a constant speed of 72 mph. Can you tell us what its average speed was for the entire journey there and back?

WORKINGS

TRIVIA

1 What is another name for the island, Rapa Nui?

2 What was the name of the well-known German archaeologist and art historian who lived from 1717 to 1768?

3 When was Boris Pasternak awarded the Nobel prize for literature?

4 What is depside?

5 Which colourless, oily, poisonous liquid was used as a war gas and has a smell like geraniums?

ANSWERS

50th | Round

LOGIC The following series of letters has a hidden underlying logic. When you have worked out what this logic is. you must replace the question mark with the correct letter to continue the series.

G E L N D J J ?

DIAGRAMMATIC In the diagram each column and row must total 25, and this includes the two main diagonal lines. Fill in the missing numbers to make this work. Here are the numbers in a random order:

7 5 3 −5 10 0 1 15 9

9	-1	8	2	7
-2				1
8				2
7				14
3	2	2	17	1

VERBAL What four-letter word will go before all of these to form three good English words?

BLACK SET FISH

MATHS What is the next number in this series?

1, 18, 4, 21, 10

MISCELLANEOUS Here is a series of letters:

H H E M ?

What letter should replace the question mark and continue the sequence?

WORKINGS

TRIVIA

1 What name was given to the Irish expatriates who gave their military service to European Catholic powers from the late 17th century to the early 20th century?

2 What was the pen-name of the author of a series of letters attacking the ministries of George III?

3 Which United States general (1860–1948) was nicknamed 'Black Jack'?

4 What was the name of the ancient capital of Media?

5 In the film *Death on the Nile*, what was unusual about the trip from Luxor to Abu Simbel?

ANSWERS

1st ROUND   ANSWERS

DIAGRAMMATIC   After 80 years. The planet has completed 16 orbits and the asteroid has completed three orbits.

LOGIC   20.

VERBAL   *MASTER*.

MATHS   33 cigarettes. When the tramp has made full cigarettes he smokes them and then makes more cigarettes from the remaining ends.

MISCELLANEOUS   After 1 minute and 52 seconds. Divide the distance by the speed of the tanker and then by the speed of the flames. Deduct the latter from the former and resolve.

TRIVIA   **1** Centaurs. **2** Emu. **3** Whist. **4** Cress. **5** Pablo Picasso.

2nd ROUND   ANSWERS

DIAGRAMMATIC   Cubes B and E cannot be made.

LOGIC   40 beans.

VERBAL   *PAR*.

MATHS   80 mph. The distance here is finite, and therefore you cannot just add the speeds together and divide by two. Imagine that the distance between the towns is 140 miles and take it from there.

MISCELLANEOUS   220. Vowels are each worth 22 and consonants are each worth 44. The values are then added together to give the total.

TRIVIA   **1** Charles Robert Darwin. **2** Bjorn Borg. **3** Malvern. **4** The Parthenon. **5** Schizophrenia.

3rd ROUND   ANSWERS

DIAGRAMMATIC   There are four ways of scoring 108.

LOGIC   M/V (1000 divided by 5 = 200).

VERBAL   *BRIOCHE*.

MATHS   6 am. Each hour is 63 minutes long. Divide the time which has elapsed since midnight by 63 and resolve.

MISCELLANEOUS   206 runs. Andy scores 60 runs, Bill scores 22 runs, Chris scores 59 runs, Dave scores 24 runs and Eric scores 41 runs.

TRIVIA   **1** Henri Toulouse-Lautrec. **2** Le Tour de France. **3** Land's End. **4** Paul Joseph Goebbels. **5** Centigrade.

4th ROUND   ANSWERS

DIAGRAMMATIC   42. Vowels are each worth 8 and consonants each worth 9. They are then totalled to give the answer.

LOGIC   No, it will sink.

VERBAL   *EERIE*. The other words are *PRIME*, *TIMED* and *HEEDS*.

MATHS   189 of each coin.

MISCELLANEOUS   One tenth. There is no need to know how many men and women there were in the town since each gender must receive the same amount of money.

TRIVIA   **1** Henry Moore. **2** Absolute zero. **3** Sikhism. **4** Occultism. **5** Dermatitis.

5th ROUND   ANSWERS

DIAGRAMMATIC   After 76 years. The inner planet will be 180 degrees in its orbit while the outer planet will be back at the start position.

LOGIC   61 cigarettes. He first makes 54 cigarettes, smokes them and then makes six from the ends. He smokes the six and then makes a further cigarette.

VERBAL   *HASTY*.

MATHS   2.1 gallons per hour. The car covers 100 miles in 2 hours 51 minutes, to the nearest minute. It ought to use 4 gallons but actually uses 10 gallons. It has therefore lost 6 gallons in the time or 2.1 gallons per hour.

MISCELLANEOUS   19 insects of each type.

TRIVIA   **1** Cello, or violoncello. **2** The phoenix. **3** Sergei Rachmaninov. **4** Ultrasonic. **5** Rudolph Valentino.

6th ROUND   ANSWERS

DIAGRAMMATIC   92. The value of the symbols on the top line reading from left to right are 24, 20, 14 and 32.

LOGIC   At the rear downstairs. The seating arrangements are as follows: upstairs—Jones, Taylor, Peters, Brown, White; downstairs—Roberts, Smith, Green, Black, Grey.

VERBAL   *VET*.

MATHS   400.75 miles. On day 1 the man covers 229 miles while on days 2, 3 and 4 he covers 57.25 miles each day.

MISCELLANEOUS   £1.75.

TRIVIA   **1** Incense. **2** Reggae. **3** Bingo. **4** Cain and Abel. **5** The serfs.

7th ROUND   ANSWERS

DIAGRAMMATIC   There are twelve ways to spell *MITRE*.

LOGIC   5.45 am. The clock stopped at 3.30 am, which is 210 minutes after midnight. The clock lost 4 minutes every hour and therefore each hour was 56 minutes long. It stopped at 3.45 am, which was two hours ago. Therefore the correct time is 5.45 am.

VERBAL   *INGEST.*

MATHS   Yes, with under one-sixth of a gallon left.

MISCELLANEOUS   Frederick again. Imagine that the speed of Frederick was 200 metres per minute. In such an instance Frederick takes 1 minute and 7.5 seconds, while William takes 1 second longer.

TRIVIA   **1** Aristophanes. **2** Mice. **3** Tonga. **4** 12. **5** Hardworking or diligent.

8th ROUND   ANSWERS

DIAGRAMMATIC

LOGIC   *U*. The second letter in the French numbers, from one to eight.

VERBAL   *AFRICA, EUROPE; PARIS, ROME; CARDIFF, LONDON.*

MATHS   10.2 runs. During his first 29 innings he scored 522 runs. After 39 innings his score was 624 runs, and so 102 runs were scored in the last ten innings.

MISCELLANEOUS   *Q*. Both top and bottom lines add up to 40 when the letters are given their numerical value in the alphabet.

TRIVIA   **1** He was a magician. **2** Horse racing. **3** Specify. **4** Hibernia. **5** Hanging or spreading strips of Anatolian cloth.

9th ROUND   ANSWERS

DIAGRAMMATIC   9. Just use simple algebra to work this one out.

LOGIC   There were three people in the syndicate and each won £449.

VERBAL   'A committee is a group that keeps minutes but wastes hours.'

MATHS   £6.47. The cheque received was for $47.06. He spent £8.24 and was left with £38.82. This was six times the value of the cheque which he ought to have received.

MISCELLANEOUS   16 minutes 24 seconds, to the nearest second. Convert the times to fractions, $1/19 + 1/24 - 1/30$, and resolve.

TRIVIA   **1** Library cataloguing. **2** Southpaw. **3** 31. **4** Birdseye. **5** Goat.

10th ROUND   ANSWERS

DIAGRAMMATIC   There are twelve ways of getting from A to B.

LOGIC   Both cars will be at exactly the same distance from London when they meet.

VERBAL   *CLOUDS, CROWDS, FEAR, HOPE, LIVE, DEAD, ROOSTS, ROASTS.*

MATHS   2 minutes 39 seconds, to the nearest second.

MISCELLANEOUS   6. The letters are the last letters in numbers, so D is the last letter of THOUSAND, and so on.

TRIVIA   **1** Sophocles. **2** Atheists. **3** Bob Dylan. **4** Dialysis. **5** 'The Angry Young Men'.

11th ROUND   ANSWERS

DIAGRAMMATIC

LOGIC   94 players taking 17 strokes.

VERBAL   *TEAR, BEAR, BOAR, BOAS, BOBS, SOBS* is one possible answer.

MATHS $(19^2 - 61)/3 = 100$.

MISCELLANEOUS   No, she only likes items whose name contains double identical letters.

TRIVIA   **1** A. A. Milne. **2** Demerara. **3** Isaac Asimov. **4** Austrian. **5** Beatrix Potter.

12th ROUND   ANSWERS

DIAGRAMMATIC   Eleven times. One collects the same four letters but in a reversed order, thus creating a different route.

LOGIC   14 whole arrows.

VERBAL   *SIDE* to give *RIVERSIDE* and *SIDEWINDER*; *MOTH* to give *MAMMOTH* and *MOTHEATEN*; *BOOK* to give *NOTEBOOK* and *BOOKCASE*.

MATHS   Yes, there is approximately one-ninth of a gallon left.

MISCELLANEOUS   Barry wins.

TRIVIA   **1** Monaco. **2** 1940. **3** Herman Melville. **4** It is a kind of pancake. **5** 147.

13th ROUND ANSWERS

DIAGRAMMATIC Rectangles C1 and A4, and D1 and D2.

LOGIC 117. The vowels in the words are each worth 15 and the consonants are each worth 24. They are then totalled to give the figures.

VERBAL *ARNOLD, BERLIN, FOSTER.*

MATHS 523.2 miles. Now that you know the answer, the way of solving it without the answer should become quite clear.

MISCELLANEOUS 8 minutes 22 seconds, to the nearest second. Convert the times to fractions and resolve.

TRIVIA **1** There was a huge volcanic eruption and the town of Pompeii was destroyed. **2** Saatchi and Saatchi. **3** An enzyme. **4** The Eiffel Tower. **5** George Washington.

14th ROUND ANSWERS

DIAGRAMMATIC Five different routes.

LOGIC
A
1:06
F
The top row of letters is made up of the first letters of the months April to August. In the second row the first number marks the position in the alphabet of the top letter while the second marks the position of the bottom letter in the alphabet. The bottom row of letters are the first letters of the days of the week, Monday to Friday.

VERBAL The countries are *BORNEO, INDONESIA* and *TONGA.*

MATHS 2 minutes 22 seconds, to the nearest second.

MISCELLANEOUS £18. Watch out for the deliberate mistake.

TRIVIA **1** Mathematics. **2** Brand's Hatch. **3** At the base of the brain. **4** Gepetto. **5** Christopher Lee.

15th ROUND ANSWERS

DIAGRAMMATIC Eleven ways.

LOGIC 4 minutes 37 seconds, to the nearest second. This is a baths and taps question with a twist.

VERBAL *NIGER, TOBAGO* and *LIVONIA.*

MATHS Jimmy was four and his mother was 28.

MISCELLANEOUS 64¼ runs.

TRIVIA **1** John Steinbeck. **2** New York. **3** Lewis Carroll. **4** It is St Patrick's Day. **5** Hercules.

16th ROUND ANSWERS

DIAGRAMMATIC 29.

LOGIC None. To get there, back and unload he would have had to have taken longer, and so we know that his lorry was empty.

VERBAL *HAM.*

MATHS £24.51.

MISCELLANEOUS 8.30 pm.

TRIVIA **1** Sherlock Holmes. **2** Intelligence quotient. **3** Desperate Dan. **4** They are the only perennial vegetables. **5** The Cresta Run.

17th ROUND ANSWERS

DIAGRAMMATIC 120 ways. Remember, *AUPAP* is neither a word nor spells *PAPUA.*

LOGIC No, she only likes numbers which contain at least one Roman numeral.

VERBAL
FLAME
LIVEN
AVERT
MERGE
ENTER

MATHS 96 of each coin.

MISCELLANEOUS 180 mph. This is not the normal average-speed question. Since we do not know the distance covered, the average has to be the out speed plus the return speed divided by two.

TRIVIA **1** Excalibur. **2** 1666. **3** *Wuthering Heights.* **4** Switzerland. **5** The Gunners.

18th ROUND ANSWERS

DIAGRAMMATIC In 8 years and 3 months. The faster planet will be 270 degrees in its orbit while the slower one will be 90 degrees in its orbit.

LOGIC 925. The letter to the left of the brackets is moved on by the number to the right of the brackets. Thus *H* is five letters from *C, E* is four letters from *A* and *U* is the next letter after *T.*

VERBAL *FAT.*

MATHS 35 mph. In this instance, imagine a distance, say 105 miles, for the journey out and also for the journey back, and then work it out from there.

MISCELLANEOUS 621 revolutions.

TRIVIA **1** A fifth. **2** Doctors. **3** Samuel Colt. **4** A kind of wood. **5** Plaster.

19th ROUND ANSWERS

DIAGRAMMATIC   169. The values of each symbol on the top line reading from left to right are as follows: 31, 36, 40 and 51.

LOGIC   £80. The number of letters in the word is multiplied by the alphabetical value of the last letter of the word.

VERBAL   *LAMB–LAME–TAME–TARE–TORE–PORE–PORK.*

MATHS   There were 31 people present, each paying £47.

MISCELLANEOUS   Yes, with nearly 2 gallons over.

TRIVIA   **1** Vitamin K. **2** The carotid artery. **3** 1954. **4** In the ear. **5** Zinc.

20th ROUND ANSWERS

DIAGRAMMATIC   Cube *C* cannot be made.

LOGIC   On the third seat from the front, downstairs, behind Mr Brown. The seating arrangement is as follows: upstairs—Green, Peters, Taylor, Jones; downstairs—Black, Brown, White, Smith.

VERBAL   *BOAT*. This gives Dreamboat, Longboat and Iceboat.

MATHS   39 gallons per hour. This one is too obvious to need explanation.

MISCELLANEOUS   'A critic is a man who knows the way but can't drive the car.' Each letter is replaced by the one previous to it and then the message is written in groups of four.

TRIVIA   **1** Munich. **2** The Sioux. **3** Osmosis. **4** A sailing boat. **5** 1953.

21st ROUND ANSWERS

DIAGRAMMATIC   There are six ways of scoring exactly 88.

LOGIC   500. The figure is obtained from the sum of the Roman numerals in the word.

VERBAL   *HAUNTED, FRIGHTENED; OBESE, WEIGHTY; SLEEPY, SNOOZE; FLIGHT, EAGLE.*

MATHS   Yes—but with only one gallon of fuel to spare!

MISCELLANEOUS   Yes, every time he cracked his whip.

TRIVIA   **1** Loose fibre obtained from old rope. **2** Guy de Maupassant. **3** Egypt. **4** Jean Harlow. **5** Kami.

22nd ROUND ANSWERS

DIAGRAMMATIC

T	C	O	M	E
O	M	E	T	C
E	T	C	O	M
C	O	M	E	T
M	E	T	C	O

LOGIC   213⅓ feet per minute.

VERBAL   The word formed is *SWIM*.

MATHS   After 10 minutes and 24 seconds.

MISCELLANEOUS   A spark.

TRIVIA   **1** Zaire. **2** Theseus. **3** Pig. **4** Deadly nightshade. **5** 1869.

23rd ROUND ANSWERS

DIAGRAMMATIC   In 232 years. The planet will have completed 16 full orbits and the asteroid four.

LOGIC   993. $D = A+G$; $E = H+B$; $F = C/I$.

VERBAL   *EAGLE, STARLING* and *HAWK*.

MATHS   Bill.

MISCELLANEOUS   His son. His grandson's grandfather is himself and his grandson's father is his son.

TRIVIA   **1** Karlheinz Stockhausen. **2** Shimonoseki. **3** Tyche. **4** The racoon. **5** In the brain or spinal cord.

24th ROUND ANSWERS

DIAGRAMMATIC   Seven ways.

LOGIC   £12,500. Imagine that there were two men and 598 women in the town. (This is just an example.) Then 166 women took their £75 worth each and a man took his £50 worth. The equation then reads $166 \times 75 + 50$ to give the answer.

VERBAL   *REVERENT, OVERSEER, NEOPRENE, NEWSREEL.* (The missing letter was E.)

MATHS   Eight scenes at 307 feet of film per scene.

MISCELLANEOUS   S. The top line of numbers totals 20 when the letters are given their values in the alphabet. The second line doubles to 40, and therefore the third line needs an S so that it becomes 60.

TRIVIA   **1** Halloween. **2** Programmable Read Only Memory. **3** Yom Kippur. **4** A third pair of legs and a second pair of wings. **5** INRI.

25th ROUND ANSWERS

DIAGRAMMATIC 81. The letters of each word are given their alphabetical value and totalled.

LOGIC Yes, the actual time is 5.30 am.

VERBAL The word formed is *LEISURE*.

MATHS You have 123 of every coin.

MISCELLANEOUS After 55 years.

TRIVIA **1** Cascade Range. **2** 1909.
3 A Malayan slashing knife with a scalloped edge.
4 Mohammed II. **5** Aswan.

26th ROUND ANSWERS

DIAGRAMMATIC One and a half black circles.

LOGIC *NORA BONE*. The numbers are a simple substitution code in which A is equal to 41, B to 42 and so on.

VERBAL
```
R  A  V  E
A  V  E  R
V  E  E  R
E  R  R  S
```

MATHS 5796 (5796/12 = 483).

MISCELLANEOUS
```
L  A  M  P
A  R  E  A
M  E  A  L
P  A  L  M
```

TRIVIA **1** The residence or office of an imperial Chinese official.
2 On the Zambia/Zaire border. **3** Lake Malawai.
4 Moamar al Gaddafi. **5** Grace Stansfield.

27th ROUND ANSWERS

DIAGRAMMATIC There are ten ways of attaining 57.

LOGIC Yes, he certainly was. The bottle is a fake, since the classification of red Bordeaux was, in 1842, as yet unheard of.

VERBAL *MONEY*, to give Moneybags, Moneymaker and Moneywort.

MATHS $((5^2 + 3^2)/2) + 23 = 40$.

MISCELLANEOUS *N*. These are the letters on a typewriter going downwards in a diagonal direction, starting at *Q*.

TRIVIA **1** Mona Passage. **2** An imaginary coin.
3 Julius II. **4** Thais. **5** An asteroid.

28th ROUND ANSWERS

DIAGRAMMATIC There are 19 ways of collecting the letters of *VENEZUELA*.

LOGIC 16 minutes each. The total listening time is 48 minutes times 2. This 96 minutes is now divided by 6, the original two listeners plus the additional four. This then gives the answer of 16.

VERBAL *TOUCAN*.

MATHS 7 minutes 20 seconds, to the nearest second.

MISCELLANEOUS 240 cans. There were 15 cans of dog food, 30 cans of cat food, 72 cans of rat poison, 60 damaged cans and 63 cans of rhubarb.

TRIVIA **1** Masaryk. **2** Papal taxation (formerly 1p) for the maintenance of the Papal See.
3 Innocent III. **4** A yellowish-brown variety of sapphire.
5 Clwyd.

29th ROUND ANSWERS

DIAGRAMMATIC

LOGIC *S*. They are the first letters of the German numbers 1 to 6.

VERBAL *KIND*, to give Gavelkind and Kindred.

MATHS No, there will be insufficient water left.

MISCELLANEOUS The missing letter is *D*. The words are therefore *DADDIES, DREADED, DISBANDED, DEMANDED* and *SADDENED*.

TRIVIA **1** A poem. **2** Grandson. **3** Nova Scotia.
4 Chrysanthemum.
5 The Danube.

30th ROUND ANSWERS

DIAGRAMMATIC In 375 of their months. The faster planet is 180 degrees in its orbit while the slower one is back at the start point.

LOGIC 84 miles. You drive for 4 hours and thus lose 17 gallons of petrol. You have therefore used only 4 gallons. You get 21 miles per gallon and therefore must have travelled 84 miles.

VERBAL *LUNGE*.

MATHS There are 165 of each of 1p, 2p, 5p, 10p, 20p and £2 coins.

MISCELLANEOUS 7 minutes 16 seconds, to the nearest second.

TRIVIA **1** Obelisk. **2** Styria. **3** Jan Ziska. **4** Pellicle.
5 A legislative assembly.

DIAGRAMMATIC There are ten ways of scoring 26.

LOGIC Smithy. John is not mentioned, so he is not guilty. Bruiser and Birdy contradict each other, and therefore one must be telling the truth. Therefore Smithy's statement is a lie and he is guilty.

VERBAL *HER.*

MATHS 68.5 runs. Multiply 18 by 16.5. Then add the 8 to the 16 and multiply this total by 32.5. Subtract the first total from this and divide by 8 to get the answer.

MISCELLANEOUS 12. Multiply the consonants in the words by 3 to get the numbers.

TRIVIA **1** Aboukir Bay. **2** White marble. **3** Taisho. **4** Praise the Lord. **5** LSD.

DIAGRAMMATIC

32	29	32	5	32
34	30	31	31	4
33	30	26	22	19
11	21	21	22	55
20	20	20	50	20

LOGIC £4.60. The values of the second and third letters are added and then divided by the value of the first letter.

VERBAL The two words are *HOPS* and *SHOP.*

MATHS 441. The first number in the brackets is the square of the first number outside them. The second number in the brackets is the sum of the first and second outside them. The third number in the brackets is the third number divided by the first number outside them.

MISCELLANEOUS 'Better free than to be a fat slave.' This version of a quotation by Aesop has been reversed and then the letters placed in threes.

TRIVIA **1** Brent. **2** Oahu. **3** Marcel Proust. **4** Immanuel Kant. **5** A light, alcoholic Mexican drink.

DIAGRAMMATIC 233. The values of the symbols on the top line reading from left to right are 64, 62, 53, 54.

LOGIC Because it is daylight. At no time did we say it was night.

VERBAL *HORN,* to give Hornbeam, Hornstone, Hornbill and Hornbook.

MATHS Multiply, plus, plus, divide.

MISCELLANEOUS *ASTER.*

TRIVIA **1** A plant-eating insect. **2** Thallium. **3** Oran. **4** Huascar. **5** Dame Ellen Terry.

DIAGRAMMATIC There are twenty ways of scoring 7.

LOGIC 1329¾ miles.

VERBAL *KICK, RICK, RICE, RILE, MILE, MULE.*

MATHS 34. The numbers are the prime numbers from 1 to 17 multiplied by 2.

MISCELLANEOUS There are 65 horses. First, ignore the final S in each word. Then take the next letter and give it its alphabetical value. In the case of pigs this is 7. However, as the series progresses for cows you use the next *two* letters, *WO*, and add these values together. For bulls you take the next *three* letters, *LLU*, and add these together. For donkeys it is the next *four* letters and for horses it is the next *five* letters.

TRIVIA **1** Khamsin. **2** The annihilation of three Roman legions. **3** 1945. **4** An American plane tree. **5** Clemens Brentano.

DIAGRAMMATIC There are thirteen ways of collecting the letters of *SKIN*. A route which can be reversed is classed as another route.

LOGIC At 10 am.

VERBAL *RANCH.*

MATHS 21 runs.

MISCELLANEOUS *AT.* They are the second and third letters of the planets in order from the sun.

TRIVIA **1** A priestess of Apollo at Delphi. **2** The brain. **3** Hatshepsut. **4** Vesta. **5** In Indonesia.

DIAGRAMMATIC

54	74	53	3	56
76	52	55	53	4
55	54	48	42	41
15	43	41	44	97
40	17	43	98	42

LOGIC 18 cigarettes. After he has made his first 17 he smokes them and makes another.

VERBAL *STONE,* to give Load stone and Stonefly.

MATHS 67.2 mph.

MISCELLANEOUS 8.15 am.

TRIVIA **1** The lowest freeman in Anglo-Saxon England. **2** Lake Trasimene. **3** Hong Kong. **4** *A Tale of Two Cities.* **5** General Galtieri.

37th ROUND ANSWERS

DIAGRAMMATIC You would need six black diamonds.

LOGIC 'When in doubt win the trick.' Each consonant is replaced by the letter following it in the alphabet.

VERBAL *LEM*.

MATHS One-third. Five hundred of the jewels were diamonds, and so the 1000 rubies remaining were only worth 200 diamonds. So there was the equivalent of 700 diamonds in all. At £200 for 25 this gives us the total earnings of £5600.

MISCELLANEOUS Yes, with one-tenth of a gallon left. Its actual speed is 9 mph and it has to cover 20 miles. It therefore takes 2.222 hours. It uses 13 gallons of fuel every hour, thus it uses 28.9 gallons in the total time.

TRIVIA **1** 'Turnip' Townshend. **2** Crete.
3 Bedrich Smetana. **4** Jean-Paul Sartre.
5 In mountainous areas.

38th ROUND ANSWERS

DIAGRAMMATIC

LOGIC 440 revolutions.

VERBAL *SPEAR* and *REAPS*.

MATHS £13.34.

MISCELLANEOUS 11 seconds. It looks as if it should take 10.8 seconds, but in fact there are not ten intervals between each stroke but nine, and so each takes 1 second. There are eleven intervals between the first and last strokes of 12, and so the answer is 11 seconds.

TRIVIA **1** Singing. **2** Jethro Tull. **3** Cyprus.
4 A humming-bird. **5** Head-hunting.

39th ROUND ANSWERS

DIAGRAMMATIC 152. The values of the symbols in the top row reading from left to right are 39, 44, 40 and 28.

LOGIC 189 insects of each type.

VERBAL *MIMOSA*.

MATHS Peter wins, but only just.

MISCELLANEOUS £25.

TRIVIA **1** Maria Theresa of Austria. **2** A functional gene.
3 Yul Brynner. **4** Richard Wagner. **5** Luzon.

40th ROUND ANSWERS

DIAGRAMMATIC Six times.

LOGIC 3606 runs.

VERBAL *OPERA*, *RESET*, *GREBE* and *EATEN*.

MATHS Divide, plus, multiply, subtract.

MISCELLANEOUS 'Morality is a private and costly luxury.' The quotation has been reversed and the vowels missed out.

TRIVIA **1** A purée of onions mixed into a thick sauce.
2 A man who drinks by himself. **3** The Jurassic.
4 An unsophisticated male negro. **5** Boris Spassky.

41st ROUND ANSWERS

DIAGRAMMATIC You would need five hearts.

LOGIC £30.

VERBAL *COMET*.

MATHS There were 70 people present, each paying £1.27.

MISCELLANEOUS *AGE*, to give Potage and Ageless.

TRIVIA **1** Henry Bolingbroke. **2** Canada.
3 Stormy petrel. **4** Howard Taft. **5** Tafilalet.

42nd ROUND ANSWERS

DIAGRAMMATIC

11	0	14	4	11
9	13	13	12	2
10	10	8	6	6
14	4	3	3	16
5	13	2	15	5

LOGIC 378.

VERBAL

```
F  I  G  H  .T
I  D  L  E   R
G  L  A  R   E
H  E  R  O   N
T  R  E  N   D
```
This is our solution, although there may be others.

MATHS Minus, multiply, plus, plus, square root.

MISCELLANEOUS 'The first casualty when war comes is truth.' The first letter and each alternate letter move ahead one in the alphabet while the second letter and each alternate one thereafter stay the same.

TRIVIA **1** Brazil. **2** John I. **3** Raymond Queneau.
4 South Korea. **5** Marston Moor.